Secret of the Rosary

Publications

To Jesus Through Mary

Berthe Petit, apostle of the Devotion to the Sorrowful and Immaculate Heart of Mary. Photograph was taken two years before her death.

The

Sorrowful and Immaculate
Heart of Mary

Message of Berthe Petit, Franciscan Tertiary

(1870-1943)

Translated from the French by a nun of Kylemore Abbey

FOURTH PRINTING, 1974
Franciscan Marytown Press
Kenosha, Wisconsin 53141

REPUBLISHED, 2004
Secret of the Rosary, USA
with permission from the Conventual Franciscan
Friars of Marytown, Libertyville, Illinois

The Sorrowful and Immaculate Heart of Mary
Copyright © 1966
Franciscan Marytown Press
Kenosha, Wisconsin 53141

Fourth Printing, 1974
Franciscan Marytown Press
Kenosha, Wisconsin 53141

Republished in 2004 with permission from the Conventual Franciscan Friars of Marytown, Libertyville, Illinois.
Secret of the Rosary
United States of America

Send all inquiries to:
customerservice@sorrowful-and-immaculate.com
vanschwer@earthlink.net
leevanschwer@hotmail.com

or to:

Editor
Secret of the Rosary
4001 N Oak Lane
Sulphur, La. 70665
U. S. A.

337-558-6523

ISBN: 1-4116-0396-6

DECLARATION

In obedience to the Decrees of Urban VIII, the author declares that for the miraculous events, visions, and apparitions narrated in this volume no other authority or belief is claimed than that which is usually given to narratives resting on merely human evidence. There is no intention to pronounce on their authenticity or supernatural character. If the appellation Saint or Blessed is herein given to any person not canonized or beatified by the Church, it is done so only in accordance with the usage and opinion of men.

Nihil obstat: John F. Murphy, censor librorum

    July 2, 1965   Milwaukee, Wisconsin

Imprimatur: ✠ William E. Cousins

    July 6, 1965   Archbishop of Milwaukee

PREFACE TO THE FRENCH EDITION

OUR LADY OF MERCY: Our Lady of Compassion: Our Lady of the Seven Dolors: Comfortress of the Afflicted — these ancient titles of the Mother of God show very clearly that the devotion to the Sorrowful and Immaculate Heart of Mary is not, by any means, a new devotion in the Church.

Cardinal Bourne has so very aptly pointed this out. "There is no question here," he writes, "of introducing a new devotion, but rather of deepening our understanding, and of giving greater force to thoughts long dear to our hearts, and rooted in the history of our race. This is why we wish to intensify our supplications to the Sorrowful and Immaculate Heart of Mary — now especially when the circumstances of our time so urgently demand it."

"Let us never forget," says the great Cardinal Mercier, "the title to our gratitude that Mary has won by Her Sorrows."

It is not to be wondered at that the new impetus to this ancient devotion has come from Issoudun, the cradle of the Archconfraternity of Our Lady of the Sacred Heart.

"By devotion to Our Lady of the Sacred Heart," writes Father Chevalier, "we thank God for His choice of Mary beyond all creatures, with a view to forming from Her virginal substance the adorable Heart of Jesus. We desire to honor more especially the sentiments of love, obedience and filial respect of Jesus towards His holy Mother. We desire to thank and glorify, by a title above all others, the ineffable power which He has given to Her over His adorable Heart. We desire to ask the Blessed Virgin to lead us, Herself, to the Sacred Heart, to obtain for us, increasingly, the abundance of graces which it contains. We desire to make reparation, through Her, and in union with Her, for the outrages done to the Sacred Heart, and to offer to the Savior our consolation for the bitterness and the sadness which were His during His mortal life."

The object of our devotion to the Holy Heart of Mary is the excellence of this Heart both intrinsically and in its relation to mankind. These two devotions, far from excluding each other, or serving a distinct purpose, are closely related and they mutually support each other.

*   *   *

When He pointed to His Heart "which has so loved men" Christ reminded us that He is in Himself in the person of the Man-God — Love, and that we can know the charity of God only through Him. We can receive and possess this charity effectively only by our union with Him and by our will to follow His example by imitating His virtues.

Amongst creatures, the one who has most abundantly received and possessed this Charity, is She who was most intrinsically united with Christ, and closely associated with His work, and who, at the same time, imitated Him most perfectly — His most Holy Mother.

She is the well-beloved daughter of the Father, the chosen Spouse of the Holy Spirit and the amiable Mother of the Word Incarnate, and our own Mother. She is also a Mother who loves, and the piety of the faithful down the centuries has paid homage to this love of Hers by honoring Her "Most Pure Heart."

It is precisely the Heart of flesh that we venerate in Mary; and through this Heart, our homage goes out to Her whole person. But the formal element of our devotion to the Heart of Mary is the love symbolized by this Heart. Her love showed itself — first and foremost towards God, and towards His Divine Son. This Son was to redeem sinners by His Sacrifice. It follows that Mary, in her love for Jesus, our Savior, proportionally loves those whom He was destined to save. All her earthly existence was orientated by this two-fold love.

On the day of the presentation of Her new-born Babe in the Temple, the prophecy of Simeon revealed to Mary that a sword of sorrow would pierce Her heart. The malice of men, which will not have them acknowledge Jesus as the Savior; the contradiction that He was to face; the malevolence of the Pharisees which pursued Him everywhere — all this would make Him suffer. But on Calvary, the prophecy would be realized to the full when Mary, the Mother of Sorrows, standing at the foot of the Cross, to which her Mother-love had brought Her, would hear Her Son confide to Her, in the person of John, the whole human race — asking Her to extend to mankind the love She had for Himself: "Behold thy son: behold thy Mother."

It is in the pain of Her compassion with the sufferings of Her Son, dying on the Cross, that the Mother of Jesus became in the full sense of the word the Mother of men. The instant this sword of sorrow was plunged into the depths of Her Heart, She adopted and loved all mankind as Her children, and She gave back Her Son to the Father from Whom She had received Him. "Father, into Thy hands, I commend His Spirit."

What title has the Sorrowful Heart of the Virgin Mother not merited to our gratitude and our love as She offers Her Son to the Father, and receives from this divine Son all mankind as Her children?

"The Heart of My Mother has the right to be entitled 'Sorrowful'," said Our Lord to Berthe Petit, "and I wish this title to be placed before that of 'Immaculate,' because She has won it Herself."

"The Church has defined in the case of My Mother, what I Myself had ordained — Her Immaculate Conception. It is My wish, now, that the right of My Mother to a title of justice be understood and universally acknowledged. She has merited it by Her identification with My sorrows, by Her sufferings, Her sacrifices, Her immolation on Calvary endured for the salvation of mankind in perfect correspondence with My Grace."

*   *   *

The dominant feature in this love of which the Heart of Mary is a symbol is Her eminent sanctity. We do not claim that sanctity is of Her essence as in the case of Christ. But She is full of Graces, the gifts of the most High! She is the Immaculate, whose victory over sin and Satan is complete, perfect symbol of a perfect love. In its relation to men, this love can have but one purpose — to obtain from God their entire sanctification by the perfect conformity of their minds and hearts with the Sacred Heart of Jesus and the Holy Heart of Mary.

Nowhere is this more clearly expressed than in the Decree instituting the Feast of the Immaculate Heart of Mary for the Universal Church: —

By this devotion, the Church renders to the Immaculate Heart of the ever-blessed Virgin Mary, the honor which is its due. Under the symbol of this Heart, it venerates most devoutly the eminent and singular holiness of the soul of the Mother of God, but, above all, Her ardent love of God, and of His Son Jesus, as well as Her maternal goodness to mankind redeemed by the Divine Blood.

*   *   *

This devotion of the Sorrowful and Immaculate Heart of Mary, when fully grasped, will have a two-fold effect upon souls.

Their love will correspond, in an ever greater measure, with the love of the Mother of God for men. They will bestow it with confidence, and above all with generosity, in imitation of Her own. Far too many of the clients of the Blessed Virgin pray to Her with the object of gaining requests of doubtful and certainly temporary futility, such as the smoothing away of difficulties, avoiding discomfort, or escaping suffering. The love Our Lady wishes to find in our hearts is a strong love like Her own — a love that subordinates all else to the doing of the Will of God. This love is exemplified in Our Lady: it was shown by the share in our redemption which She accepted on Calvary.

Ours must be a reparatory love. United with the Mother of Mercy — like Her and with Her — we shall offer satisfactory reparation to the Heart of Jesus for our own sins and for those of the world. "Let me mingle tears with Thee mourning Him Who mourned for me. All the days that I may live" (Stabat Mater).

"It is in hearts that a change must be effected. This will come about only through the devotion (to the Sorrowful and Immaculate Heart) understood, expounded, preached and recommended everywhere."

This conversion of hearts, demanded by Our Lord from Berthe Petit, has been incessantly requested by His Divine Mother in recent apparitions at La Salette, Lourdes, Fatima and Beauraing where the emphasis was on penance.

But has not the world, alas, remained deaf to these motherly appeals? Here is the explanation of the fact that the bitter trials of today, far from teaching their lesson of reform, serve but to plunge mankind into greater disorder and chaos.

However, beyond the lowering clouds and the darkening horizon, the star of hope, founded on the promises of the Sacred Heart, "I shall reign in spite of Satan, and the enemies he incites," is still shining in the firmament.

"I confess," wrote Cardinal Pie, "that up to the present our misfortunes have not made us better. . . . In spite of this, none the less, the more I apply myself to the close scrutiny of the thoughts of the Savior in our regard, the more convinced am I in predicting that soon there will come an abundant effusion of Mercy. And the sources from which I am drawing this confidence embolden me to believe that in uttering these words, I am inspired by the Spirit of God."

*   *   *

This reign of the Sacred Heart, the reign of Mercy, will be established when men abandon the odious impiety of materialism that now exists and when the expiatory love of penitent hearts will turn towards Our Lady "to reanimate Faith and Hope in the world."

She has, Herself, revealed to Berthe Petit that "it is with a steadfast will that My Son wishes souls to have recourse to My Sorrowful Heart. I am awaiting this conversion in souls, My Heart overflowing with tenderness, asking nothing better than to pour into the Heart of My Son what is confided to My own, and to obtain graces of salvation for all."

When hearts will be changed by the beneficent influence of the Devotion to the Sorrowful and Immaculate Heart of Mary, who is it that will speak to the Heart of Her Son, if not She Who will place Her all-powerful supplication between the offended Jesus and the sinner? Is it not Her mission to bring two hearts together — the Heart of Jesus burning with the flames of the most ardent Love, and the heart of the Christian, too often tepid if not icy cold? Who will obtain this outpouring of graces on the world, if not She Who has the key of the Heart of Jesus, the untarnished source of all graces?

Assuredly, for those who have recourse to the all-powerful suppliant, the treasurer of the Heart of Jesus, OUR LADY OF

THE SACRED HEART, there is no cause beyond hope in this world.

*   *   *

The reign of the Sacred Heart through Our Lady of the Sacred Heart, is the end towards which the devotion to the Sorrowful and Immaculate Heart is surely leading.

The heroic life of Berthe Petit who was the "apostle" of this devotion, her example, and the expression of her innermost thoughts cannot fail to lead readers of this book along this Marian way — the royal way that leads to the Heart of Jesus, source of all peace and happiness.

TH. CADOUX, M.S.C.
Superior of the Mission,
of Kaolack Senegal.
(formerly Provincial-Superior of France).

*   *   *

"The grace of Her Immaculate Conception, together with the initial fullness of Charity, considerably heightened in Mary that capacity of Hers for suffering from the greatest of all evils which is sin. Souls suffer thus in the proportion of their love for God Whom sin offends, and of their love for souls whom mortal sin turns from their high destiny only to deserve eternal damnation."

"The Immaculate Heart of Mary was, therefore, Sorrowful in the very measure it was Immaculate and all-pure: in the measure with which the initial plenitude of Charity never ceased to grow in Her, until the moment of Her death."

"When we say 'Immaculate Heart of Mary' we recall that which She received at the moment of Her conception; when we say 'Sorrowful Heart' we recall all that She has suffered and offered for us, in union with Her Son — beginning with the words of the aged prophet Simeon up to the day She stood beneath the Cross on Calvary, and until Her own most holy death, shortly before Her Assumption."

R. P. GARRIGOU-LAGRANGE, O.P.

PERSONAL CONSECRATION

Composed by Berthe Petit

Sorrowful and Immaculate Heart of Mary, dwelling pure and holy, cover my soul with your maternal protection so that being ever faithful to the voice of Jesus, it responds to His love and obeys His Divine Will.

I wish, O, my Mother, to keep unceasingly before me your co-redemption in order to live intimately with your Heart that is totally united to the Heart of your Divine Son.

Fasten me to this Heart by your own virtues and sorrows. Protect me always.

CONTENTS

CHAPTER I

PREPARATION FOR HER MISSION

BERTHE-FRANCES-MARIE-GHISLAINE PETIT was born at Enghien in Belgium on January 23, 1870. She was the third daughter of Monsieur Petit, an attorney, and of his wife Jeanne, neé Meys. The child had inherited a delicate constitution.

From her earliest years the Divine Master was pleased to shower upon her His favors and to mark her with the seal of the Cross. At the age of four, a first vision of the Blessed Virgin rapt her in ecstasy. A little later, in the Chapel of the Sisters of the Union of the Sacred Hearts, she beheld the tabernacle open wide and the Infant Jesus coming towards her. Signing her forehead, He said:

"You will always suffer, but I shall be with you."

She made her first Communion at the age of ten, with the greatest fervor. "I received Jesus," she wrote, "with the most ardent desire of loving Him more than all, and with all the simplicity of a child I besought Him for a religious vocation, never doubting that it would be granted. After Holy Mass I said to the Sister, who often reminded me of it: 'It is decided; I shall be a religious, and because I must be like Jesus, I shall suffer much.'

'Who told you that?' asked the Sister.

'The little Host I received which was my wonderful Jesus.' Since then I have lived on the thought of being a religious."

The little girl liked, naturally, as all children do, to run about and play. Later on she delighted to tell of the fun she had skating on the lake in the property of the Duke of Arenberg. Indeed she excelled in this particular sport. There were also marvelous games of hide and seek in the great Park open to certain families of the town. One day in company with some friends she fell from a horse in full gallop and was dragged along for several yards.

In 1884, her health became a great trial. Typhoid fever brought her to death's door. Given up by the doctors, she lay for several weeks between life and death. She was anointed, but when she was given Holy Communion she was almost unconscious. She would recall, later on, how she felt a great shock and saw a dazzling light, before falling back into coma. Her mother, in an act of heroic faith, set out for Lourdes. On her return, the child's life was saved, but her health always remained precarious.

This gifted child was filled with veneration for the priesthood and the thought of Christ making Himself present during the Holy Sacrifice of the Mass, under the appearance of bread and wine in the hands and at the word of His priests, in order that He might immolate Himself mystically to His Father for the benefit of mankind, was to her the source of ever increasing wonder.

At the age of fifteen one day during adoration there came to her the thought of offering her pains and sufferings for souls and, above all, for the *sanctity* of priests. "Each time I assisted at Mass," we find in her notes, "I said: 'My Jesus, may your minister never offend you in anything.' It was my dream to be one day a missionary. My tears fell fast, abundant and sorrowful at the thought of souls who were being lost. I had but a vague idea of the misery here below, but Jesus sweetly disposed my heart to the apostolate which I was to understand much later. I thought much, at that time, of the Sisters of St. Vincent de Paul. Their devotedness to souls attracted me. I lived for a long time with this thought, but as events proved, it was never to be realized."

Berthe had received an excellent education at the convent of the Bernardine Dames of Esquermes who were by now established at Ollignies. To quote one of her companions at the boarding school: "Her piety was profoundly touching without ostentation. She was very delicate in health, gentle and resigned. She was like a beautiful delicate flower. There was something at once other-worldly and ideal in her character — a contrast to the boisterous joy of her companions."

"My last year at the boarding school," Berthe writes, "passed quickly. I was grieved to be leaving the monastery. I had often been ill — even gravely." During an attack of peritonitis she received the Holy Oils for the second time. "With what devotedness I was nursed! I can see again those gentle, anxious faces watching my slightest sufferings in order to relieve them. Piety was a great source of consolation for me, and I spent many happy hours permeated with the things of

God."

"During evening prayers in the study hall I could see from my place the lamp burning before the Blessed Sacrament. This was my delight! . . . Often I was scolded for not answering the prayers. My whole heart went out involuntarily towards the Blessed Sacrament. It was an intimate prayer, sweet and meditative, that arose from my heart and often I shed tears of emotion. The nun in charge, a holy soul whom I have since much appreciated and loved, often kept me back when the other pupils had gone, and asked the cause of my tears. I could never explain it to her, and many an evening I was reprimanded. I remember feeling this keenly. I had a deep and intense desire to belong to God alone and it was this that impelled me to seek the Prisoner of Love."

Berthe was almost eighteen years old when she left Ollignies. "You are taking away everybody's heart," said Dame Marie Hortense, "and you are leaving yours to none." Indeed her heart belonged to God alone.

The same Religious spoke thus of her pupil twenty-three years later:

"Berthe Petit was a boarder at Ollignies during the years 1886 and 1887. She was a pious, virtuous girl, delicate of manner and bearing. In those days her health was already very precarious and this prevented her from studying as assiduously as she would have liked."

"I have remained in touch with her since she left school. I always found her very supernatural, accepting trials of health or any others with a perfect submission to the Will of God. She was even happy to suffer for love of Our Lord. She is very reserved on the question of her interior life and she has no pretensions to high spirituality."

"When her parents suffered a great reverse of fortune, she devoted herself to them in every way. Her filial love stopped at nothing; she became not only their breadwinner, but their moral support. After days of hard work she would muster sufficient strength to spend part of the night writing in order to help her father in his office work."

"The marvelous thing is that Berthe has been able, for twenty years, to maintain this laborious task in spite of severe suffering and in the absence of nourishment. She has often been at the last extremity. She surmounted each of her maladies: but they made her increasingly weaker, and ever less capable of working, but always courageous and disposed to accomplish whatever Providence might ask of her."

"I may also mention, especially, her influence over those around her. To see her is to become attached to her and to seek her advice. Her kindness, her obliging charity, full of modesty, touches one deeply; her one wish is to help, to relieve, and to do good to souls."

A retreat at the monastery of Esquermes, given by the Reverend Father Tesnière, threw fresh light on her vocation and, from then on, she wanted nothing better than to know the Order of St. Vincent de Paul. Later on came hesitations; contemplation attracted her and she now thought of the Servants of the Blessed Sacrament of Angers.

She had her parents' consent not to appear in society before her twentieth year, but family parties were very numerous and very animated; music was the attraction. Berthe sang and played the piano delightfully. Both her sisters were married at this time. One of them settled down in Canada and was to be the mother of twenty-two children.

Suddenly, like a bolt from the blue, the horizon darkened. . . . Heavy financial losses made a complete change in the easy circumstances of the attorney and his family. Now the dream she had when a girl of sixteen became a reality. It had left a vivid impression upon her; she had seen herself working for her livelihood at night, by the light of a lamp. . . .

Now came the decision to sell the home and to leave Enghien and settle in Brussels.

"On September 8, 1888," she writes, "I found comfort in an act of supreme abandonment. In the church of the Capuchin Fathers I went to confession and Father Godefroid (her director) said to me: 'It is all over, my poor child, it is evident that your vocation is now to be with your parents in their misfortune. You wanted to consecrate yourself to God in the convent. Instead, you will devote yourself to them, but that will not prevent you from being the spouse of Christ. You will be a crucified spouse. Go and tell that to the Blessed Virgin.' "

"I knelt down at the feet of our Lady of Grace and from my heart I cried 'O Mary, my good Mother, speak to Jesus of my sacrifice and of my abandonment to His Divine Will. But ask Him, O my Mother, that the sacrifice of my vocation may be the source of yet one more priest. In the place of a poor religious, may there be to console your Son a holy, fervent priest who will bring Him many souls!' "

"I went back to Father Godefroid and told him of the longing of my soul. He blessed me, adding 'Your prayer will be heard and perhaps you will know it one day'. . . ."

Berthe's Father

In the great city Berthe began her hard life's work. Nothing had prepared her for it and her health was very precarious. But her courage sustained her. She was exceedingly deft, and in spite of her inexperience she found work, thanks to Father Jarlan, a Blessed Sacrament Father. He had become her director and recommended her to various people. Now orders came for First Communion crowns and Berthe worked at them late into the night. . . . The dream of long ago!

Little by little people began to be interested in her. Gifted as she was with a very beautiful voice, she sang the solos in the Church of the Fathers of the Blessed Sacrament, Chaussée de Wavre. Friends were anxious that she should go to the conservatoire and, eventually, take up theatricals! Her confessor, however, opposed this, and directed her towards the work of teaching. Berthe, who was well educated, became, thanks to her intelligence and perseverance, an excellent tutor. For two years she was visiting-governess to several young girls. Her life was extremely hard. Up at five, she assisted at Mass, attended to household duties and then set off on foot, never taking a tram so as to save the fare. She was satisfied with a little bun for her hasty lunch, after which she went back to her pupils, returning home in time to prepare the supper. She would play the piano to give pleasure to her parents and then spend part of the night correcting exercises.

Berthe's Mother

"Two years went by — years which now would seem impossible to relive," she wrote in her diary, "so painful were they. Providence helped me. I worked for my loved ones. They began to take up their life again and they gained new courage for the struggle. They knew nothing about my secret sufferings. I had found a sweet repose before the Blessed Sacrament. My sacrifice was made and Jesus gave me ever more the conviction that a priest would be given me for my sacrifice, my crucifixion. I worked; I was suffering bodily all the time and there was often sorrow in my heart, even in my soul. But God gave me grace to fulfill my duty and I felt great peace.

6

My life was very full, my strength was worn out and I suffered more and more. But how happy I was to be the only one to suffer! My dear ones were increasingly consoled by the friendship of noble hearts. Mine alone was crushed. I was an exile in a world now smiling upon me. But I avoided it as much as I could, for it was a source of perpetual torture to me."

As a matter of fact, an illness — an acute attack of rheumatism — forced Berthe, who now received Viaticum for the third time, to give up her work as governess.

Prosperity returned by degrees to the family circle. Monsieur Petit, who had been appointed liquidator to an attorney in Brussels, now began to initiate his daughter in his law affairs. She collaborated with him in a work on legacies which is still consulted by the legal profession. Berthe's intelligence and her balanced mind were remarkable in this domain, and she gave her advice with that sagacity and prudence, conciseness and clarity which she brought to bear, all her life, on her judgments spiritual and temporal. Here is a typical example of her mentality and one which might well serve as a guiding principle: "You must not attempt, by tactless or ill-timed remarks, to surpass the good you have set out to do."

For a long time she had offered herself as a voluntary victim for the priesthood, and now she felt called to consecrate this dedication by a solemn vow, on the feast of Christmas 1893. In the next chapter will be seen the marvelous way in which the Divine Master was to recompense her.

In 1895 she lost her director, Father Jarlan, who was called to Paris on December 17, 1910. Here is what this religious thought of her.

We set out his judgment textually, for it shows to great advantage the work of grace in her soul.

"I declare that I was the spiritual director of Berthe Petit from the year 1888 to 1895. When I first saw her she was eighteen years of age. She had just left the boarding school and was devoting herself to her parents who were then enduring a very severe trial — the loss of their fortune. From that time her life was one of suffering and heroic devotedness. She made every effort to procure some comfort for her beloved parents and to make their lot more bearable. She forgot herself to the detriment of her own health. Several times I saw her at the point of death, but the moment she recovered she would take up her life of sacrifice once more, although she knew that she was thereby exposing herself to relapses."

"Her patience during these illnesses has been admirable; she had special devotion to the Divine Will which she wishes to accomplish perfectly. She is a chosen soul, very high in the ways of God. She thirsts for suffering and her one ambition is to be a living victim, holy and agreeable to God according to the mind of St. Paul."

"Her intelligence is lively, her judgment sure, her prudence remarkable."

"She is very anxious for the sanctification of others. Often I used to put her zeal to the test by confiding to her some souls in whose conversion I was interested. I always had reason to rejoice or rather to thank the Author of every gift for having given such grace to a soul whom I regard as privileged."

"None of the souls whom I confided to her resisted her gentle influence. Two, especially, having led a stormy life in the world, entered religion and there died the death of the predestined. I have often been told that souls are irresistibly penetrated with respect in her presence. However, she does nothing to attract this deference. Her bearing is elegant but withal very simple, her manners are affable and her conversation perfectly natural."

From 1895 to 1908 one illness followed another and these were so grave that the patient received the last Sacraments three times. They were, in the opinion of the doctors: — endocarditis, jaundice, abscess of the liver with vomiting, angina, hemorrhages and even tuberculosis was feared.

After the departure of Fr. Jarlan, Berthe confided her soul to Fr. Bouffé. At that time she took part in all the works of the Blessed Sacrament Fathers and, when Fr. André was Superior, he appointed her, under the name of Sister M. Madeleine of the Cross, directress of the Confraternity which he founded.

Thenceforward her time was no longer her own. People called at all hours to ask her advice, her help for the ailing, her instructions for associate members, so much so that there came a day when she felt quite exhausted. Seeing herself obliged to neglect her home duties, she resigned this office.

In 1896, Fr. Masselis, Rector of the Redemptorist Fathers, became her director and remained so until 1908, the year he set out for Rome. He said in 1910:

"In my humble opinion, here is a soul singularly favored by God, and since I have known her, very faithful in following the impulse of grace. I have found in this chosen soul real and profound humility, absolute purity of heart, invariable obedience and patience that I do not hesitate to call heroic."

"A prey from her youth to bodily infirmity, she has never ceased to suffer, but she has suffered unflinchingly the most acute, often the most atrocious pain. To these sufferings were added heartaches, above all from the day she saw her parents ruined. Thenceforward she devoted herself to them, working unceasingly, despite the extremely painful condition of her health."

"For long years, this generous soul had offered herself by vow for the conversion of sinners and I could never say that her spirit of sacrifice wavered before these extraordinary trials with which God was pleased to visit her."

"She was by nature gifted with a lively and well-trained intelligence, a highly balanced judgment and a generous heart. She used these gifts only in self-forgetfulness and devotedness to others."

"Nothing more discreet than her words, her conduct: nothing more dignified than her bearing: nothing more gentle than her behavior: nothing more edifying than her whole life. She exercised, too, an exceptional influence over those who had to deal with her, and amongst the pious and judicious people who had contact with her (I know a great many) I think that none could be found who did not recognize in the life of Berthe Petit, the seal of real sanctity. Oftentimes Our Lord made her the instrument of His mercy to souls who had strayed away."

"Christian prudence guides this soul who is surely led by grace and I declare that, despite her bodily sufferings and interior trials, this virginal soul, trained in the school of the Holy Spirit, always enjoyed the precious fruit of real and profound peace."

"She is unaware of her merits and this saintly unknowing, which I witnessed so often, and which it was my duty to foster, has revealed the fund of humility with which this soul is endowed. That Our Lord was pleased to shower astonishing favors on her does not at all surprise me."

"By nature calm, well balanced and devoid of all exaltation, she has received these divine favors without being in the least troubled or disconcerted by them; and while no one was more astonished at them than herself, she has but one end in view: to know and accomplish the Holy Will of God as manifested to her."

Being warned against any mistaken piety she took advice also from a well-known Carmelite, Fr. Stephen, who set her at ease with regard to her state of prayer.

In 1898 she benefited by a legacy, left her by a cousin, and she had the immense joy of being able to offer to her parents an attractive house in the rue du Cornet (Etterbeek). According to an intimate friend "good taste reigned everywhere — in the pictures, drawings, embroidery, tapestry, in all you could discern the brush, the pencil and the needle of her who was the soul, or rather the driving force, which was expending its whole energy in the service of others."

When she was under the direction of Canon Boone, her parish priest, she began, in spite of all her sufferings, to teach catechism to the children, to care for the sick and to encourage by word and by correspondence a vast number of souls.

That same year brought her another joy; she made her first pilgrimage to the Grotto of Massabielle. From Lourdes she went to La Sainte Baume, which left an inexpressible memory with her. She had special devotion to St. Mary Magdalen whose name she had taken when she belonged to the Confraternity.

In 1899, as a result of further hemorrhages, the doctors, fearing the onset of the dreaded tuberculosis, ordered a journey to the South and Berthe set out with her friend (Miss C.) for Italy and Sicily, returning by the Italian and Swiss Lakes. These "sixty days," as she called them, were unforgettable. She kept an account of the journey in a charming little album, artistically illustrated with dried flowers. Her descriptions are fresh, witty, full of originality, and they breathe great elevation of soul.

When she returned home her lungs were healed!

On their way back by Venice the two travelers visited St. Mark's and, admiring the treasures of the sacristy, they came face to face with Cardinal Sarto and asked his blessing.

"Where are you ladies from?" he asked, with a very pronounced Italian accent.

"From Belgium, your Eminence."

"Ah! Belgium," said he, "what a fine country — very christian! People pray very much there. May God protect that land!"

Berthe Petit, 39 years of age

He looked attentively at Berthe, and making the sign of the cross on her forehead, said to her: "Listen carefully, my child, to the voice of God. He has designs upon you."

This was indeed a prophetic utterance from him who was to become St. Pius X.

From 1900 to 1908 summer tours succeeded one another in the company of that same friend whose secretary Berthe had now become. The itinerary included the banks of the Rhine, Oberammergau, Austria, Bohemia, the Tyrol and Switzerland together with two further pilgrimages to Lourdes.

Meanwhile, the trials of her health continued unrelentingly: heart attacks, stomach ulcer, periostitis of the tibia, etc.

From this time (1908), at the age of thirty-eight, the inability to absorb food became evident. Her stomach, as we have said, was always very delicate and the doctors never succeeded in overcoming what they called "anorexy." For years, they prescribed remedies, but these served only to aggravate her case. In despair, they inflicted on her a "gastric lavage" which proved unfortunate and provoked an ulcer that never healed.

It has often been asked whether the servant of God suffered from hunger. She did not. She had a consuming thirst, but she never complained of the lack of food. Her weight never varied and although she had all the appearance of a fragile and delicate person, she was by no means a skeleton.

She lived thenceforward, from the age of thirty-eight to seventy-three, on a cup of black coffee in the morning — always rejected an hour afterwards — a little white wine in the afternoon and, at bed-time, a glass of water containing the juice of half a lemon. Towards the end of her life, when her strength was failing, the Divine Master requested her to try to take some solid food. She forced herself then, in obedience, to absorb a spoonful or two of thick vegetable soup, but the taste of all food, however agreeable, was nauseating and she dreaded it. She retained the Eucharistic Bread alone, and the only hunger she felt was for this divine food. When the priest, who brought the Blessed Sacrament in the morning, happened to be late, it was a real suffering to her, and Good Friday was a day of bitter agony. [1]

She would perhaps have obtained, through the influence of her powerful friends, the privilege of receiving Holy Communion that morning, but in the spirit of mortification, she did not wish to ask for it.

When people spoke to her of her condition, she would change the conversation: it was repugnant to her to be an object of attention. God alone knows the unpleasantness she

---

[1] In those days the faithful were not allowed to communicate on Good Friday except when in danger of death.

had to put up with in the hotels, when on tour, by her refusal to partake of any food!

Often did she beg the Divine Master to make her existence "normal," in order precisely to avoid indiscreet curiosity and malevolent suppositions. "I am thy real nourishment," He said to her at the beginning of her fast, when He forbade her to make any further vain efforts to take solid food. At Loreto in 1910, He insisted in this wise: "Do you know that I, and nought beside, am your life?"

It is true that the state of habitual fast, in itself, adds nothing to the sanctity of the apostle. It is willed by God and it is not for us to question the divine ways of dealing with souls. On March 30, 1916, Jesus said to her: "In your mission of making known the Sorrowful and Immaculate Heart of My Mother, your fasting has not been the essential point in proof of the timeliness of the Devotion or the justice of the title for which I wish a foremost place when appeal is made to my intervention. I wished to be your sole nourishment. For My Love has so ordained it: My Providence so designed it."

CHAPTER II

THE "PRIEST OF HER LIFE"

If Berthe had already many proofs that she was an object of love on the part of her Divine Master, still more did she experience this on Christmas night, 1893. The occasion was her making of a vow as victim for the priesthood, and the place the Church of the Fathers of the Blessed Sacrament in Brussels.

The text of the vow is as follows:

"O Jesus, Victim for ever immolated in the Holy Eucharist, I, Mary Magdalen of the Cross, prostrate myself at Thy feet, feeling more than ever the need and the grace to abandon myself, following Thine example and through the guidance of God, in order to become a victim with Thee, and through Thee. I renounce myself, my tastes and my satisfactions, and I willingly consent to become in Thy Hands an ever docile instrument. I offer myself to Thy Sovereign Majesty and resign to Thy Will my whole being with each of my faculties. I abandon my own will to acquiesce fully in Thy good pleasure. I dedicate myself willingly and with love as Thy servant and Thy slave, to submit to Thy divine plan. I hold myself ready at Thy first call, when Thou seekest a heart to comfort Thee and to share in Thy sorrow, in Thy disgrace and in Thine apparent failure with souls. Finally, I surrender myself to Thee to be totally dedicated to Thy workings — to be the insignificant instrument in which Thou concealest Thyself, whilst having full sway to lead and direct everything."

"In this spirit, O Jesus, and leaning in all confidence upon the arm of the Blessed Virgin Mary, Thy Immaculate Mother and Thine incomparable Handmaid, I pronounce before Thy Divine Presence in the Blessed Sacrament, the vow to accept spontaneously and of my own free will the trials, the sacrifices, the humiliations and desertions which may befall me."

"I make this vow with the special intention of being a voluntary victim of Thy justice and Thy love, but especially, O my Jesus, if Thou acceptest my sacrifice, for the soul of 'The priest of my life.'"

"Permit me, O my Victim-Jesus, ever to draw nearer by Thy sacramental life and to quench Thy burning thirst for my perfection and for the salvation of souls! And now, O my Master, my God, grant me ever to be faithful to the holy obligations which I have contracted for love of Thee!"

"O Mary, Mother of Sorrows, Mother of my Jesus and my own sweet Mother, watch over me, pray for me, bless me."

"O my beloved Patroness, Saint Mary Magdalen, and St. John, best beloved of the Apostles, watch over me, help me, intercede for me and present me to Jesus and to Mary."

Elsewhere in her notes we read:

"No words could convey the happiness which penetrated my heart at that moment, and the utter detachment which lifted my soul to Him Who, more than ever, will be my only Love. To love Him without measure, ever more, even in the midst of disappointment, bitterness and sorrow, giving Him all; reserving nothing to self; to be *crushed* in the divine mill — this is my only desire, the object of my life."

But let us follow her in her solemn prayer:

"My God, I belong to Thee, accept me as Thy ever crucified victim, dispose of Thy Magdalen and grant her the grace to be ever faithful to Thee. I offer myself, O Jesus, for the priesthood; for priests and if my prayer of 1888 has been heard, I offer myself, as I have never ceased to do since the 8th of September, for that special priest I begged then of Thy Divine Mother, Our Lady of Grace."

Her notes give us further light:

"These words, uttered at the moment when Jesus was in my heart, plunged me into a state which I cannot describe and which I shall remember eternally. Lifted up above all earthly things I spoke to Jesus in my soul. It was at the Elevation. When I had adored Jesus in the Sacred Host and in the Chalice, I raised my eyes to the Monstrance, penetrated with an intense feeling of love and sacrifice for Him Who was willing to accept my poor and miserable soul as victim. The Monstrance was now no longer visible: an enormous cross appeared in its place. My Jesus was nailed to it, and at the foot of this cross stood Mary, my Mother, with John the be-

15

loved Apostle. . ."

"Oh! what sorrow in the attitude of the Blessed Virgin! What compassion in the unforgettable features of St. John! An inner voice whispered to me: 'Thy sacrifice has been accepted, thy petition granted. Behold thy Priest: thou wilt know him one day.' "

"My eyes were riveted on this vision. I contemplated my crucified Master, my Mother and St. John whose features were engraved on my memory. [2] I gave myself to Jesus, confided myself to Mary, and begged the Apostle to inspire me with his ideals and with those of Mary Magdalen, my holy patroness."

"Little by little, all vanished and there remained but the cross alone, the bare cross. 'Magdalen, I accept thy donation. . . Thou shalt be a victim!' "

" 'O Jesus, may it be especially for the priest of my soul!' "

" 'Thy life is for him, thy sufferings have saved him. . . Here is the cross which I offer thee. It is heavy, but I shall bear it with thee!' "

"I know not how long I was immersed in this colloquy during which I told my Divine Master of my desire to console His Heart — for the priesthood, for souls, for all He would ask. The first Mass was over, the second already well advanced. It seemed to me that I was returning from afar. There I was — a poor miserable soul annihilated by the divine goodness which inundated my heart with heavenly joy!"

This luminous cross was seen also by two friends of Berthe, one of them, Marie B. . . . , died, according to her wish, at the age of thirty-three; the other, Lydia R. . . . , became a nun in the Convent of the Servants of the Blessed Sacrament at Angers.

Now, it happened that he who was to become Berthe's priest, was at that very moment sub-deacon at the High Mass which was being celebrated at Vincennes on Christmas night. He was, therefore, at the left of the celebrant, as St. John had appeared in the vision on Christ's left at the foot of the Cross. But Berthe was to know him only fifteen years later.

On the 14th of May, 1907, Berthe was at Lourdes for the third time. To use her own expression, "she had been called

---

[2]   St. John, perfect type of the priesthood.

here" by Our Lady who spoke to her thus on arrival at the Grotto: "My Son loves His crucified spouse. We both love you. You will know the member of the priesthood who has responded to your sacrifice." On the 16th of that same month Berthe suffered agonizing gastric pains. After Mass Our Lady told her to drink water from the miraculous fountain and the pains lessened somewhat. That same afternoon Our Blessed Lady said to her: "Love your sufferings; they console My Son. You will suffer always."

As Berthe was leaving Lourdes, the Immaculate Mother added: "Come back again, my child, I will help you."

Thus it happened that the following year, which was the Golden Jubilee of the Apparitions at Lourdes, we find this predestined soul at the hallowed sanctuary. Here, Mary confirmed her promise: "You will see the priest whom you begged from God, twenty years ago, and the meeting is close at hand."

Back in Belgium in July, 1908, Berthe no longer hoped that the meeting would take place in this world. She had fallen very gravely ill, and received once more the last Sacraments. She was now 38 years of age.

From this time on, as has been already remarked, she could no longer retain any nourishment: her stomach absolutely refused all food except the Holy Eucharist.

On September 4th, Christ encouraged her in these words: "Your sufferings have won, and will continue to win, an abundance of graces. Be always a ready victim! Accept with more courage the cross of life! You can still help *the priest whom you are soon to know.*"

Three weeks later, Berthe, now convalescing, was seized with an ardent desire to return to Lourdes. Her friends did their utmost to dissuade her from undertaking this journey. Father Masselis, her confessor for the time being, was the only one to encourage her. So she set out.

Breaking the journey at Paris, she received Holy Communion in the Church of Our Lady of Victories, where she heard Our Lord say to her: "I wish to gratify your long waiting, because of your suffering in which your only desire was to accomplish My Divine Will: you shall meet your priest."

Berthe and her friends had hardly boarded the train for Lourdes when a priest entered the compartment to find a vacant place for one of his penitents. He exchanged a few polite words with the travelers, and then withdrew. *Without a moment's hesitation Berthe had recognized the very features of St. John whom she had seen at the foot of the Cross on that memorable Christmas night of 1893. Those features were engraved in her memory*; she was looking at them now; she was radiant and thanked God for this wonderful grace.

A month later, the same priest arrived in Lourdes where, by a strange coincidence, he had arranged to take up residence in the hotel where Berthe and one of her friends happened to be staying. Stepping from the train, he met them as they were going to hear Mass. He recognized them and saluted, suggesting that they assist at his Mass which he would offer for their intentions in the Chapel of the Rosary Hospice. Later on he was to write: "Never was I more intensely conscious of the presence of God as I was from the very beginning of that Mass."

Frequent mention is made in the life of Berthe Petit of a similar grace granted to priests who celebrated Mass in her presence.

At the moment of the Elevation, Jesus revealed Himself to His servant, and she heard these words: *"This is the priest for whom I have accepted your sacrifice; My mother and I bless you."*

Three days later, the Divine Master ordered her to reveal her secret to this priest whom He had chosen, and Our Lady said to her: "What my Son desired is being accomplished."

Who was this priest selected by Our Lord at the request of Berthe? His name was Louis Decorsant. He was of French nationality, born at St. Quentin in 1866; his mother was from Alsace. He had not intended to become a priest, but a lawyer. Having gained high honors in his university course, he received the diploma of Doctor of Law in Paris and was at this time contemplating marriage. One day, as he was praying before a Pieta, suddenly and convincingly he felt the call to the priesthood. Bidding farewell to the young lady he loved he did not hesitate from that time forward to give himself entirely to Christ. He made this sacrifice sixteen days after Berthe Petit had requested Our Lord for one more vocation to the priesthood — and prayed that she might know this priest one day. It was the exchange for her own sacrifice.

Louis Decorsant had just been made an officer of the reserve when he decided to take up his priestly studies in Rome. There he obtained his Doctorate in Philosophy and Theology. On his return to Paris he was ordained priest by Cardinal Richard in the Chapel of the Catholic Institute, on the 9th of July, 1893.

Appointed assistant curate at Vincennes, he ministered there for fifteen years, bringing many souls back to God by his labors in pulpit and confessional. In addition, he wrote several books on Catholic sociology and apologetics.

But gradually overwork undermined his health and he was compelled to resign his curacy at Vincennes. He was now looking for a chaplaincy in a convent, and with this end in view, he went to Lourdes to implore light and guidance from Our Lady. We have just seen how, and through whom, the Mother of God enlightened him.

Through various providential circumstances Father Decorsant left Lourdes in company with Berthe and her friend. While they were assisting at his Mass at the Basilica of the Sacred Heart, Montmartre (Paris), the Savior said to Berthe: "Be faithful to My grace: My work will be accomplished."

With all his uncertainties now dispelled Father Decorsant decided to act. After the due canonical procedure, he took leave of his Superiors in France, and set out for Brussels. Here, with full ecclesiastical sanction and all faculties for his priestly functions, he took up his residence in a Convent Guest-House. His health was very precarious and he was obliged to give up parish activities of every kind. Nonetheless, he was much appreciated by religious communities and was in constant demand for conventual sermons and confessions.

Under the general direction of Father Masselis, he became the spiritual guide of Berthe Petit. He was thus the instrument of Divine Providence acting as intermediary between her and the ecclesiastical authorities in regard to the messages entrusted to her for communication.

When, later on, Berthe was granted the privilege of a private oratory, Father Decorsant became her chaplain.

CHAPTER III

THE MISSION

Our Lord had given His servant to understand long before, that He wished her to prepare herself for a special mission to be assigned to her in due time. On August 4, 1909 it was made known to her that St. Catherine of Siena would be one of her special guides. Later on, St. Michael was given as second patron.

It was during the Mass celebrated by Father Decorsant on Christmas Day, 1909 that Berthe Petit had the first revelation regarding this mission.

She beheld the divine and wounded Heart of Jesus and, adhering closely to it, was the Heart of Mary pierced with a sword. Then she heard these words: "Teach souls to love the Heart of My Mother pierced by the very sorrows which pierced Mine."

This same vision and these identical words were repeated on December 31, 1909 and on January 30, 1910.

On February 7, 1910, Berthe saw in vision the Hearts of Jesus and Mary in close contact and surmounted by a dove, symbol of the Holy Spirit. At the same time she heard these words: "You must contemplate the Heart of My Mother, as you contemplate My own; live in that Heart as you wish to live in Mine; give yourself to that Heart as you give yourself to Mine; spread the love of Her Heart which is wholly united to Mine."

On the following day, the two Hearts were shown to her with their projecting rays of light and Our Lord said to her: "I have made known to you the wishes of My Heart concerning the Devotion to the Heart of My Mother. Love it and make it loved! This love will be for you and for the whole world a source of grace, and it will bring upon you great blessings. Surrender yourself to My love. The pressing desire of My Heart is about to be confided to you . . ."

A few days later, on pilgrimage to St. Anne's in Alsace, it was revealed to Berthe that her mission would be the *Consecration of the World to the Sorrowful and Immaculate Heart of Mary.*

As she continued her journey in the company of her

mother and of Father Decorsant to whom her father had confided Berthe (for Mr. Petit had died on December 2, 1909) she arrived in Italy where, at Siena, a great and marvelous surprise awaited her. She was making the Holy Hour in her room, when suddenly a brilliant light appeared, in the midst of which was Saint Catherine of Siena. Placing on Berthe's head a crown of thorns, the Saint said to her: "Wear this as I did! . . . It is the wish of Divine Love. Obey: this Love wills that I protect you."

This apparition of the glorious patron of the Third Order of St. Dominic sheds a heavenly light on the fraternal affection which binds together the evangelical Father, Dominic, and the seraphic Father, Francis. This bond their numerous children have perpetuated ever since in a tradition of brotherly love. From this time on, we see, united in Jesus under the same diadem of Love, Berthe, later to become the humble Franciscan Tertiary, and the Dominican Tertiary, Catherine of Siena, a saint of the court of heaven.

Next morning, while Father Decorsant, her spiritual Father, was celebrating Mass in the saint's room, Berthe saw, at the moment of the Elevation, a magnificent radiance and in it the Face of Our Lord crowned with thorns. She heard these words: "The world must be consecrated to the Sorrowful and Immaculate Heart of My Mother as it is to Mine. Fear nothing, no matter what obstacle or suffering you may encounter; your only object must be the accomplishment of My Will."

The travelers reached Rome on Easter Sunday. During the Mass celebrated by Father Decorsant in the Chapel of St. Louis at the French Seminary, the Hearts of Jesus and Mary, closely united and surmounted by a dove, appeared once again to Berthe and she heard the following words: "This wish of Mine follows from what I accomplished on Calvary. When I gave John to My Mother as her son, did I not confide the whole world to Her Sorrowful and Immaculate Heart?"

Then the Savior ordered her to make a sketch of the vision of the two Hearts. "I shall guide your hand," He said. In obedience to this command Berthe reproduced what she had seen — the sketch which is given in these pages.

On June 3rd, the message was repeated as follows: "It is My desire that this picture, guided by My hand, be spread far and wide, simultaneously with the invocation. Wherever it will be venerated, My Mercy and My Love will be made manifest and the sight of Our Hearts, wounded by the same wound, will encourage tepid and weak souls to come back to their duty."

During the Holy Hour of the 24th to the 25th of August, Our Lady appeared to Berthe showing Her wounded Heart.

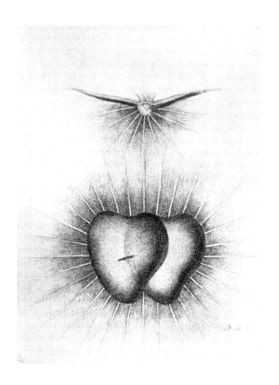

Sketch of the Vision of the Two Hearts

In September, Berthe went to Lourdes with the National Pilgrimage. There she met the Reverend Father Bulliot, Marist, ex-professor of the Catholic Institute of Paris. We see, from his own attestation, the impression the humble pilgrim made upon him. He says:

"My first meeting with Berthe Petit was in one of the chapels adjoining the Rosary Basilica at Lourdes. She and her mother assisted at the Mass I celebrated there. During the whole of that Mass I felt the deepest impression of confusion for my sins that ever I experienced. I saw them in a different light and I promised Our Lord to confess them again in a new general confession. Imagine my surprise when, after Mass, Berthe Petit said: 'During Mass I heard a word which concerns you: "Pray for him, he will soon feel the effect of your prayer." ' She gave me some words of encouragement which, I felt, were appropriate and which appeared to me to come straight from the compassionate Heart of Our Lord."

"I remained under that impression for several weeks and I noticed the calm, the humility and the sweetness with which this child of God spoke to me. It was obvious that she was fully aware of the striking connection between my impressions and her words."

"I mention this only by way of expressing an opinion formed on my own experience."

"How happy I should be if her desire were realized — that of the Consecration of the World to the Sorrowful and Immaculate Heart of Mary!"

On the 17th, Saint Catherine of Siena appeared once again to Berthe and said: "Jesus confided a mission to me. To further it I endured many a painful hour. I have known mockery and contempt: I have seen incredulity deny the divine workings. You have been chosen for another mission which will meet with every kind of obstacle, but which will triumph later, for the Master wills it. Be resigned to everything and have unfailing confidence."

As a result of a warm recommendation from Father Masselis in February, 1911, Cardinal Mercier of Malines had been brought in contact with Father Decorsant and his spiritual child. His Eminence was immediately won by the beauty and the orthodoxy of the Devotion. He did not hesitate to grant, on March 30, 1911, an indulgence of 100 days, toties quoties (i.e. each time), to the invocation: "Sorrowful and Immaculate Heart of Mary, pray for us who have recourse to Thee."

This gesture was eventually to prove of the utmost importance. The wishes of Our Lord, together with the sketch of the two Hearts, were communicated to His Holiness Pope Pius X.

In a letter to the Belgian Primate written with his own hand, the Sovereign Pontiff said in conclusion: "Your Eminence has exercised the privilege of granting 100 days' indulgence to the ejaculation. I would ask that the pious lady be content with this for the present."

Events were indeed to prove that, at the outset, the progress of the Devotion was to be in a slow measure.

On the following June 17th, Mary appeared again to Her servant whose sufferings in the meantime had redoubled, and the Mother of God said: "See here the wound of My Heart, similar to that of my Son, and the torrent of grace ready to gush forth from it . . .". And Our Lady showed her a multitude of people of every race and color: the sick and the infirm. All were praying with arms extended; some were being cured, others were falling upon their knees, suddenly converted. It was like a regeneration of the world. . .

In conclusion, the Blessed Virgin said: "Do not allow any trial, any disappointment, any suffering to discourage you."

After Holy Communion on September 8th, the Savior added this important announcement:

"The Heart of My Mother has the right to be called *Sorrowful* and I wish this title placed *before* that of *Immaculate* because She has won it Herself. The Church has defined in the case of My Mother what I Myself had ordained — Her Immaculate Conception. This right which My Mother has to a title of justice, is now, according to My express wish, to be known and universally accepted. She has earned it by Her identification with My sorrows, by Her sufferings: by Her sacrifices and Her immolation on Calvary endured in perfect correspondence with My grace for the salvation of mankind."

"In Her co-redemption lies the nobility of My Mother and for this reason I ask that the Invocation which I have demanded be approved and spread through the whole Church. It has already obtained many graces; it will obtain yet more when the Church will be exalted and the world renewed through its Consecration to the Sorrowful and Immaculate Heart of My Mother."

On September 17th, Our Lady appeared again, her brow wounded and bleeding, her hands and Heart pierced. By those sacred stigmata, Mary showed how much She identified Herself with the sufferings of Jesus; and while the servant of God was, more than ever, interiorly enlightened on this Compassion, Mary said: "You can now understand the sorrows which my Heart endured, the sufferings of my whole being for the salvation of the world."

During the Holy Hour from the 24th to the 25th of March,

1912, Mary deigned to add: "I have called myself the Immaculate Conception. To you I call myself Mother of the Sorrowful Heart. This title willed by my Son is dear to me above all others. According as it is spread everywhere, there will be granted graces of mercy, spiritual renewal and salvation."

The year 1913 brought Berthe an increase of sufferings: she had an attack of pleurisy, followed by severe gall trouble.

On the Feast of St. Joseph (that year transferred to April 2nd) Our Lord said to her: "Joseph, who supported My Mother and protected My divine Infancy, is your support in a cause which is so dear to him, because he knew many of the sorrows which transfixed My Mother's Heart, and he foresaw, before his death, all that Her Heart would still have to endure."

In 1914, a miraculous event took place in Berthe's life, and it may be opportune to mention it here, for it serves to show how deeply she was steeped in the supernatural. The chief witness was a Dutch lady, Miss de K. . . . , then on a visit to Madame Petit and her daughter.

At this particular time Berthe was suffering acutely from an ulcer on her foot, with periostitis. The doctor had pronounced the case very grave. All night long they placed on it compresses of Lourdes water. During the Holy Hour, Our Lady appeared to the patient and reassured her saying: "You have only to have recourse to me for help." Later on, the Mother of God returned and blessed Her servant. The ulcer had disappeared, leaving only a white outline, the trace of which remained until the end of her life.

Miss de K. . . . relates of the agony she endured that night by reason of her anxiety for the patient, until falling asleep, she dreamt she saw Berthe cured and the wound covered by a white scar. Next morning, she hastened to Berthe saying: "Is it true that you are cured, and that a white tissue now covers the wound?" "Yes," replied Berthe, "I am cured."

When acquainted with these facts by Father Decorsant, Cardinal Mercier replied: "What you have written to me is edifying. The cure of the dear patient in such extraordinary circumstances proves that God is with her. It is evident that she is being sustained by grace, to bear this long martyrdom with serenity."

CHAPTER IV

THE GREAT WAR

It is interesting to note that the supernatural events in Berthe's life were in close relation with the social and political crises which agitated the world during the first twenty years of this century.

It was in no small measure owing to this that Berthe Petit was able to win over eminent ecclesiastical personages to the Devotion of the Sorrowful and Immaculate Heart of Mary.

In view of the terrifying pronouncements that follow — predictions made by Our Lord to Berthe Petit — let us state clearly at the outset that neither political animosity on the one hand, nor distortion of fact on the other, is involved here. The misfortune that fell on the German people as a consequence of the First World War resulted, as everyone knows, in the evolution of a regime which had certain good features, but which, as a whole, gave rise to a system of repression at home, and to greed for conquest abroad. This is one of the main causes why the fate of Europe is still in the balance.

The German people themselves, numbers of whom were the foremost victims of the Nazi movement, are the first to see these events in their true light. As an instance of this, it is significant that when a translation into German of Berthe's life was proposed, the German editors insisted that the message should be given integrally. They asserted that, thus and thus only, will the messages from Heaven bring healing — not to Germany alone but to the whole world!

The first, and indeed one of the most striking, of her supernatural communications concerning world events, took place shortly before the war of 1914-1918.

It will be remembered that, in 1912, the celebrated Eucharistic Congress, at which the Emperor of Austria-Hungary was present, took place in Vienna. On the 12th of September during her thanksgiving Our Lord made this announcement to Berthe:

"A two-fold murder will strike down the successor of the aged Sovereign, so loyal to the Faith. This will be the first of events, grievous but expedient to My designs, which will precede the chastisement . . ."

As it happened, the horizon midway in 1914 clouded over abruptly. On June 28th, the heir to the throne of Austria-Hungary, the Archduke, together with his wife, was assassinated at Sarajevo.

The following day, Our Lord said to Berthe: "Now begins the onward march of coming events, which are going to lead you to the great showing of My Justice."

Nevertheless, thousands of pilgrims once more assembled in Lourdes to celebrate yet another Eucharistic Congress. The atmosphere was heavy with foreboding. It was the month of July and there were anxious hearts . . .

In his book entitled *The Sacred Heart of Mary* Fr. Lintelo says: "A humble demand was submitted to His Holiness Pope Pius X. It seemed to many that the City of Mary was particularly apt as the place for the consecration of the human race to the Immaculate Heart of Mary. This consecration, if made by the Papal Legate at a world-wide reunion of prelates, priests and faithful, might arrest attention by the accompanying splendor and unanimity which would guarantee lasting results. But the hour of Divine Providence had not struck. With profound wisdom, the Holy Father judged it more expedient to reserve this solemn act for some purely Marian solemnity."

Pius X, who was a saint [3], did not then consider the moment opportune for the consecration of the world either to the Immaculate Heart of Mary, or to Her Sorrowful and Immaculate Heart.

The winter had proved a very painful one to Berthe, with the result that a change of air was found necessary. In spite of the political upheaval, she planned a journey to Switzerland. The Divine Master had told her to fear nothing, but to seek repose where circumstances would indicate. In July, 1914, Berthe and her mother, accompanied by Father Decorsant, went to Sarnen, near Lucerne. On the 28th of the same month war was declared on Serbia. Frontiers were immediately closed and it was impossible for the travelers to return to Belgium.

God so willed it. Here is what He said to Berthe on the

---

[3]   Beatified and later canonized by Pope Pius XII during the Marian Year (May 1954).

29th of July concerning the German Emperor, William II: "His ungovernable pride has unleashed a scourge the extent of which cannot be foreseen. He will authorize, in My Name, every kind of ravage, caused in reality, by his own hatred and ambition. But I will break his might and his pride. Heaven will be the reward of the innocent victims and many a soul will turn to Me forever . . ."

Our Lord spoke once more to His servant on the 6th of August: "I curse the arrogant people who slight Me and who persecute the true Faith using the while My Name and authority. Any nation that prepares its military forces in advance to hurl them unjustly upon the choicest portion of God's flock, pursuing, albeit for the purification of souls — its ruthless way like a murdering scourge of destruction, is not the nation of My choice. I shall break it and chastise it because, in its insane pride, it refuses to see its own religious and moral decay. It is in the crushing of this pride that My punishment will be manifested."

Meanwhile, events were being precipitated and while the thunder of the battle raged, the Almighty called to Himself, on August 20th, His servant, Pope Pius X. Berthe had been forewarned of his death a year previous.

On the morning of that same day, the Germans entered Brussels.

On the 3rd of September, the conclave gave as successor to Pius X, Cardinal Giacomo della Chiesa who took the name of Benedict XV.

At this time, Jesus, speaking of the Kaiser, said to Berthe: "I will crush the hypocrite who continues to pose before Me, making it appear that his injustice and cruelty have the seal of My assent." And on the 10th of September, a little more than four years before the prophecy was realized, He added: "A chastisement will strike down the ambitious one on the very soil he has now unjustly invaded . . ."

About this time, Father Decorsant wrote to the newly elected Pope, through Cardinal Mercier, who had just assisted at the conclave. Recounting the steps already taken in the reign of Pius X, the letter concluded with the following revelations made by Our Lord to his spiritual daughter:

"The worst calamities which I had predicted are unleashed. The time is now ripe and I wish mankind to turn to the Sorrowful and Immaculate Heart of My Mother. Let this prayer be uttered by every soul: '*Sorrowful and Immaculate Heart of Mary, pray for us.*' Let this prayer dictated by My Love as a supreme succor be approved and indulgenced, no longer partially and for a small portion of My flock, but for the whole universe, so that it may spread as a refreshing and purifying balm of reparation that will appease My anger."

"This Devotion to the Sorrowful and Immaculate Heart of My Mother will restore faith and hope to broken hearts and to ruined families: it will help to repair the destruction: it will sweeten sorrow. It will be a new strength for My Church, bringing souls, not only to confidence in My Heart, but also to abandonment to the Sorrowful Heart of My Mother."

On the 20th of September, it was Our Lady who appeared before Berthe to tell her: "It is with an unshakable resolve that my Son wills souls to have recourse to my Sorrowful Heart. With my heart overflowing with tenderness, I am awaiting this gesture on the part of souls, that I may reiterate to the Heart of my Son whatever will be confided to my own Heart, and thus obtain graces of salvation for all."

We shall see later on how the Holy Father responded to this two-fold wish of Jesus and Mary.

Circumstances brought about the visit to Switzerland of the Reverend Father Frey, Superior of the French Seminary in Rome. It is interesting to hear his impression of Berthe Petit whom he met in Fribourg. We quote his statement here together with that of Father Bohrer, Chaplain of the Institute of St. Agnes at Lucerne.

"I had occasion to see Berthe Petit at Sarnen, from the 8th to the 12th of August, 1914. I saw her again at Lucerne, from the 7th to the 10th of October of the same year."

"No one ever made an impression on me such as I experienced on meeting her. It seemed to me that I was in the presence of a being more than human. I always found her most recollected and dignified — yet without excess — for she was unfailingly affable. A smile of welcome would light up this countenance, so emaciated, so ravaged by suffering."

"Her conversation was earnest, and she was remarkable for her tact and delicate attentions to those around her: on occasion she would laugh heartily, yet with restraint. Something pure and heavenly emanated from her whole person and commanded respect. I never knew her to fail by the least gesture or word contrary to the most exquisite sweetness, the most delicate charity, the most scrupulous modesty."

"She was ever ready to bestow her kind attentions on her mother who did not even appear to notice them. In everything she acted with utter self-forgetfulness, without the slightest affectation but with utter simplicity."

"She always showed the deepest reverence and the most complete obedience to him whom she called 'Father'. She loved solitude and prayer, and yet she never hesitated in the continual sacrifice of her own taste, in order to give pleasure to her mother or to those with whom she lived."

"For nourishment, I have seen her take a little black coffee with a lump of sugar in the morning. Later, at midday, and occasionally in the evening, she took a little white wine."

"As I was giving her Holy Communion, I noticed that her tongue, heavily coated, was split in the center. She must be suffering from a horrible thirst."

"She has assured me that in one full week she sleeps only about three hours, and at that it is a very light sleep during which she does not completely lose consciousness."

"Her piety is touching: I have seen her, after Holy Communion, with her arms modestly crossed on her breast and head slightly bowed, remaining completely motionless for more than three quarters of an hour. Seeing her thus, one gets an indefinable impression of peace and happiness. It seems as though she were, for a few moments, free from all sufferings, and completely absorbed in God."

"Her sincerity is above all suspicion. In this regard one could not, honestly, have the least mental reservation. It would be doing that soul atrocious injury. Her countenance is open and limpid, without the slightest embarrassment. What she says, she believes with all her soul. When you speak to her about the Devotion to the Sorrowful Heart of Mary, she expresses herself in such a tone of conviction that the listener is entirely convinced. I shall never forget the tone in which she said to me: 'Ah! How much I feel that Our Lord wants to see the Sorrowful Heart of His Mother loved and honored!' You have the conviction of absolute trust in her assertions. Anything like an untruth on her part, would appear an impossibility."

"On the other hand, she is a soul who realizes fully the import of her words. She seems to me to be extremely intelligent. What strikes me specially about her, is the perfect moderation and balance of all her gestures and words. She is never carried away, or unduly hurried. Her judgment is remarkably sure: perfect equilibrium reigns in all her faculties. She is completely self-possessed in all her actions and words. When you remember that she suffers perpetually a real martyrdom from constant headaches, stomach ulcer, burning thirst, etc., you have to admire her serene composure."

"There is no trace of exaltation or gushing enthusiasm about her. She is ruled not by imagination, but by intellect."

"She is perfectly conscious of her exceptional role, and she accepts it, solely because she is convinced that such is the Will of God. She declares that she accepted it only with the greatest repugnance, having begged God to leave her in her obscurity. She has few consolations in her surroundings, and her extraordinary mission brings her only sufferings."

"She says that, of all the crosses Our Lord has placed upon her, this is the heaviest. No matter how deeply you search, you cannot discover any personal motive for the task she is assuming. She asks no better than to be broken, crushed, annihilated — provided that the Sorrowful Heart of Mary be glorified as Jesus wishes."

"To sum up: Confronted with this insoluble problem, you have to admit that you are dealing with a saint and that her statements are to be taken as entirely trustworthy. Furthermore, the moment you come in contact with her, any prejudices you may have had against her, vanish."

It may be opportune here to quote the statement of Father Bohrer, Chaplain to the Institute of St. Agnes at Lucerne, who wrote thus on the 3rd of December, 1914:

"Since the year 1911, I have seen Berthe Petit on several occasions. She was staying in Lucerne with her mother. I have often been received by these ladies, but for the past two months I have had occasion to be in closer contact with Berthe. She was obliged to remain temporarily in Lucerne, for the war had prevented her return to Belgium."

"It is quite obvious that her life is a series of perpetual sufferings, physical and moral, which give her no respite. They are capable of completely crushing one who takes no solid nourishment, but only a little black coffee in the morning and a very small glass of wine at midday. Even this her stomach rejects almost immediately. Yet, this invalid is regularly up and about all day, doing the housework, surrounding her mother with constant care, going out on needful but very fatiguing errands, receiving people who come to her for light and consolation; praying and writing. She is always calm, always affable, always recollected, always eventempered."

"As for her nights, I can well believe one so truthful and straightforward as Berthe as well as those in her immediate circle when they assure me that the night always means a long and painful insomnia, broken only by a quarter of an hour's sleep. It is easy to see this, for the next morning, Berthe would present herself at the Communion bench, more worn out and crushed physically, than at any other time of the day. However, after Holy Communion, she appears invigorated and ready to begin another full day such as I have described."

"I have sometimes enumerated the various Christian virtues — with this soul in mind — and I cannot but testify that she possessed them all in an eminent degree."

Here is the opinion of the Reverend Father Garrigou-Lagrange, O.P., Professor of Theology at the Angelicum (Rome).

ROME, OCTOBER 4, 1951

"I have a vivid remembrance of Berthe Petit whom I saw in Switzerland during the 1914-1918 war. I much appreciated the Devotion to the Sorrowful and Immaculate Heart of Mary. It recalls — as was the viewpoint of Cardinal Mercier and Cardinal Bourne — what the Blessed Virgin has received from God — the grace of Her Immaculate Conception; and also what the Mother of God has done and suffered for us. This invocation seems opportune in these days of universal suffering, as borne out by the consecration made to the Sorrowful and Immaculate Heart of Mary by several Bishops in various dioceses throughout France and Belgium."

A soul so contemplative and, at the same time, so active as Berthe Petit might well expect that the demon would interfere and make obstacles to this Devotion which is directly contrary to his interests. Actually, he worked with all his might against it. According to Miss de K. already quoted, the "evil one" gave signs of his presence before the war, tossing the furniture of the house upside down and dragging chains on the staircase. At Lucerne, on the 13th of December, 1914, things were still worse. The three travelers had rented a flat there. That same day as Berthe was leaving the Collegiate Church where she had prayed for the cause so dear to her heart, she heard a voice hissing with fury: "I will wage war against you to the end, by obsessing minds, hardening hearts and feeding passions!"

Turning around abruptly, the servant of God saw no one. Continuing her prayer, as she was going down some steps which led to a landing, she felt herself pushed with an irresistible violence. She was thrown down eighteen stone steps, and she felt instinctively that she would be killed on the spot, or else broken in every limb. She was shockingly bruised but managed to stand up. She was obliged to go to bed for eight days. "Bear all for the cause and for your country," said the Divine Master with unutterable sweetness during her Holy Communion next morning. No doubt, she was paying already for the great joy which awaited her at the end of the month of May, 1915 . . .

On the 31st day of that month, eight days after Italy had entered the war, Benedict XV, postponing the Consistory over which he was to preside, substituted his discourse by a letter to the Dean of the Sacred College, Cardinal Vanutelli. It concluded with the following recommendation addressed to all the Bishops of the world: "Let us send up our prayers, more than ever ardent and frequent, to Him in Whose hands lie the destinies of all peoples; and let us appeal with confidence to the *Sorrowful and Immaculate Heart of Mary,* the most gentle Mother of Jesus and ours, that by Her powerful intercession, She may obtain from Her Divine Son the speedy end of the war and the return of peace and tranquility."

This was a first acknowledgment by the Holy Father in response to the petitions which had been sent to him. He even amplified this gesture by granting, on September 28th, an indulgence of 100 days "toties quoties" to the invocation and this at the request of Cardinal Granito di Belmonte, ex-Nuncio of Brussels [4] who had become a fervent apostle of the Sorrowful Heart. The Sovereign Pontiff, however, did not judge any

---

[4] He was the Papal Legate of Pope Pius X — later Saint Pius X — at the Coronation of King George V, June, 1911. Monsignor Pacelli, later to be Pope Pius XII, was a member of the Papal mission.

more than his predecessor, the time opportune for a world-wide Consecration.

In his pastoral letters of June and September, 1915, Cardinal Mercier recommended the faithful to pray to the Sorrowful and Immaculate Heart of Mary. In January, 1916, the Belgian Primate left for Rome, where he remained more than a month. On his return journey he stopped at Lucerne and gave an audience to Berthe Petit in the Hotel National. Next day, the Primate offered the Holy Sacrifice for her in her presence. Later at the station, while awaiting the arrival of the train, he had a long conversation with her. Finally, stepping into the compartment reserved for him and his Vicar General and successor, Msgr. van Roey, His Eminence stood up and blessed the servant of God as the train steamed out.

During the month of February, Our Lord said the following words to Berthe: "It is through the Sorrowful and Immaculate Heart of My Mother that I will triumph, because having co-operated in the redemption of souls, this Heart has the right to share a similar co-operation in the manifestations of My justice and of My love. My Mother is noble in everything, but She is especially so in Her wounded Heart, transfixed by the wound of Mine."

"Desiring for Her Heart a radiant, dazzling, brilliant triumph, I have awaited this time of universal distress which finds an echo in the Sorrowful Heart of My Mother, a Heart universal as My own. To adopt this Devotion and to spread it, is to accomplish My Will and to respond to the wishes of My Heart. Because, by prayer and by the consecration made to this Heart, graces of light will be obtained. They will gradually bring souls to the full knowledge of our united Hearts, which have been wounded by the same wound, the inexhaustible source of all good for humanity, and the glory of which is now, and ever will be, the happiness of the elect for Eternity."

In the pastoral letter of Cardinal Mercier on March 7th, following his return to Belgium, we read:

"Our Holy Father the Pope asks that the mothers and widows now in mourning would stand on Good Friday with the Mother of Jesus, at the foot of the Cross, and unite their sacrifice with the bloody sacrifices of the Redemption. All of us will enter into these sentiments of His Holiness. Belgium has already been consecrated to the Sacred Heart of Jesus

Cardinal Granito di Belmonte

Taken from a photograph inscribed to Berthe Petit, "to Mlle. Petit, child of the Sorrowful Heart of Mary, Mother of God." Rome, November 1, 1925.

+ J. Card. Granito Pignatelli di Belmonte; Bishop of Albano.

and to St. Joseph. On Good Friday we shall consecrate ourselves to the Sorrowful and Immaculate Heart of Mary. We are happy to honor the Immaculate Conception of the Blessed Virgin and we do well; but besides this gratuitous privilege granted by God to Her who was to become His Mother, do we not forget the title to our gratitude which Mary acquired by Her sorrows? Pierced as She was by the sword of Her interior martyrdom, the Heart of Mary willingly associated Her own compassion with the immolation of the Divine Victim of Calvary for the redemption of our souls."

"The evil hours that we are enduring invite us, in a special way, to have recourse to the mediation of Our Lady of Sorrows. Fulfilling therefore, the ardent wish which has been expressed to me, I shall consecrate in the very depths of my soul, during the Office of Good Friday, our Diocese, and in the limits of my power, our dear Country, to the *Sorrowful and Immaculate Heart of Mary.* I exhort the priests to unite their intentions to mine, and the faithful to repeat devoutly the invocation to which I have already granted an indulgence of 100 days: *Sorrowful and Immaculate Heart of Mary, pray for us who have recourse to Thee."* [5]

His Eminence greatly encouraged the Devotion to Mary Mediatrix, and in this connection our Lord said to Berthe: "To you I assign My Mother as supreme Mediatrix through Her Sorrowful Heart."

---

[5] This passage of the Pastoral Letter of Cardinal Mercier is mentioned in the Reverend Fr. Lintelo's pamphlet: "The Sacred Heart of Mary," p. 73. On page 96 we read "O Sorrowful and Immaculate Heart of Mary, in the name of Thy love for Jesus, in the name of Thy ineffable mercies for mankind, hasten the reign of the Sacred Heart in the world."

CHAPTER V

THE ROLE OF CARDINAL BOURNE

Cardinal Bourne, Archbishop of Westminster and Primate of England, was the first to realize and to fulfill in so far as was possible for him (i.e. in the religious though unofficial sphere) this "ardent wish" for the greater benefit of his country. Instructed by Reverend Father Condamin, S. J. [6] on the 1st of May, 1916, the Primate understood at once the importance of the matter. Not only did he grant an indulgence of 100 days to the invocation, but he prepared the way for a solemn consecration in accordance with the demand made by Our Lord.

In his letter of September 3rd, Cardinal Bourne gave thanks to God for the victories obtained on the Marne and on the Yser. He then pointed out that, even with increased military strength, there was still need of powerful help to defeat the enemy. He wrote:

> "It has ever been the practice of the children of the Catholic Church to beg in all their cares and anxieties the help and intercession of Her Who was privileged to stand by Her Divine Son dying on the Cross, and we desire today to exhort you, dear Reverend Fathers and dear children in Jesus Christ, to place all your prayers and supplications under the protection of the Sorrowful and Immaculate Heart of Mary. Jesus Christ Our Lord might, had He so willed, have dissociated His holy Mother from the sorrows and awful sadness of His Passion and Death. Such was not His Will. Having bestowed upon Her by His own free choice, in view of Her Divine Motherhood, that complete immunity from original sin, which we name Her Immaculate Conception, He willed to ask Her acceptance of the fullest share in His sufferings for our redemption, that it was possible for any creature to receive. That acceptance She gave freely, unhesitatingly, and in fullest measure, for our sake; and thereby merited from Her Divine Son a place and power of intercession that belongs to Her alone."
>
> "We should fail to honor duly Her Divine Son, were we to

---

[6] See the footnote at the end of this chapter.

forget and fail to honor, praise, and use the power which He has willed to bestow upon Her in return for the Sorrows which united Her Heart so closely and so intimately with His in the supreme sacrifice of His life."

Then recalling the tender devotion of the English people through the Catholic centuries, the Prelate went on to say:

"Nowhere in Christendom should honor be paid more readily to the Sorrowful and Immaculate Heart of Mary than here in England. Of old, in the days of united Faith, Her purity and Her Sorrows were ever held in loving veneration. In those days England was in very truth Our Lady's Dowry."

"It is therefore, not with the idea of introducing any new devotion, but rather in order to give fresh meaning and greater force to thoughts long cherished by us all, and deep-rooted in the history of our race, that we desire to consecrate this renewed effort of prayer, which the special circumstances of the moment so urgently demand, to the Sorrowful and Immaculate Heart of Mary."

With this end in view, Cardinal Bourne prescribed the prayers to be said on Friday, September 15th, Feast of Our Lady of Seven Dolors, or on the Sunday following, in honor of the Heart of Mary, venerated under Her two-fold title: "In order that," continued the Cardinal, "by this act of public homage, honor may be given to the Son Who is dishonored if we fail to recognize the dignity and power which He has seen pleased to bestow upon His most holy Mother."

In the issue of September 17, 1916, "La Croix" of Paris noticed that the day, September 15th, Feast of Our Lady of Dolors (chosen as a result of a divine message as the date on which for the first time ever public prayers in honor of the Sorrowful and Immaculate Heart of Mary were to be recited) had marked the highest success of the British Army.

The Archbishop of Westminster begged Father Condamin to ask for the formula of the Act of Consecration: "I have asked Berthe Petit," replied Father Decorsant, "to obtain it during one of her thanksgivings." Jesus deigned a favorable hearing to His servant and dictated to her the following prayer which the Cardinal, according to Father Condamin, "found very beautiful, simple and to the point, perfectly noble and dignified." — "How could one be surprised," added Cardinal Bourne, "considering its origin? "

We quote the text of the formula exactly as it was sent to England:

ACT OF CONSECRATION TO THE SORROWFUL AND IMMACULATE HEART OF MARY

O Lord Jesus Who, on Calvary and in the Holy Eucharist, hast shown Thyself to us as the God of love and mercy, kneeling humbly at Thy feet we adore Thee and beg once more for Thy forgiveness and for Thy divine pity on the third year of this unexampled war.

And remembering that, by Thine own act on Calvary, the human race, represented by Thy beloved disciple John, gained a Mother in the Virgin of Sorrows, we desire to honor the sufferings and woes of our Mother's Heart by devoting ourselves to it in solemn consecration.

It is but just, O Mary, that our souls should strive henceforth to venerate thee with special homage under the title of thy Sorrowful Heart — a title won by sharing in the whole Passion of thy divine Son and thus co-operating in the work of our redemption — a title due to thee in justice, and dear, we believe, to Jesus, and to thine own Heart wounded by the wound in His.

We consecrate, therefore, O Mary, to thy Sorrowful and Immaculate Heart, ourselves, our families, our country, and those who are fighting for its honor. Have pity upon us; see our tribulations, and the anguish of our hearts in the midst of the mourning and calamities that lay waste the world. Deign, O Mother of God, to obtain mercy for us that, being converted and purified by sorrow, and made strong in faith, we may henceforth be devoted servants of Jesus Christ and of His Church, for whose triumph we pray. O Mary Immaculate, we promise to be faithful clients of thy Sorrowful Heart. Intercede for us, we beseech thee, with thy Son that, at the very cry of thy Sorrowful and Immaculate Heart, His divine Power may speedily bring to pass the triumph of right and justice.

Sacred Heart of Jesus, have pity upon us.

Sorrowful and Immaculate Heart of Mary, pray for us and save us.

*   *   *

In his pastoral letter, dated from Rome in 1917, the Primate of England instructed his clergy in regard to the public recitation of this Act of Consecration to which he had granted 200 days indulgence. This was done on the first Sunday of Lent and again on the 30th of March, Feast of Our Lady of the Seven Dolors.

"I wish," said Our Lord at this time to Berthe, "that My apostle Francis (Cardinal Bourne) make the Solemn Consecration of his country on the Feast commemorating the day when, as the fruit of the joyful and the sorrowful 'Fiat' of My Mother, I appeared in the world as the Savior of the human race (Christmas, therefore)."

Once again the Archbishop of Westminster fulfilled the wish of the Divine Master. The Consecration was celebrated with great solemnity in all the parishes of Great Britain. This homage of a solemn consecration was rewarded in a remarkable way. The British Army obtained, time after time, notable victories.

These "notable victories" are confirmed in a rather curious way in the "*Memorial du Maréchal Foch.*" — "I could never repeat it too often," he writes (page 51), "that the English fought in a most extraordinary way. *They won victory upon victory.* At the beginning of October they had broken the formidable Hindenburg line at its strongest point. *But still more wonderful, these victories were won almost unknown to themselves. They did not seem to be aware of it. . .*"

This is a purely military testimony, above suspicion and therefore all the more impressive. For when writing these lines, Marshal Foch was obviously not in the least concerned with establishing a link between the *strange* character of these English victories and the fervent prayers of the British Catholics, at the humble request of a Belgian woman, of whose existence the Marshal knew nothing whatsoever.

However, the year 1918 brought something other than success in the military arena. At one time it seemed that catastrophe was at hand. It was then that His Eminence, at the demand of Our Lord, had the Consecration renewed for the third time, on March 29th. What had happened? . . .

In a letter to Father Condamin (April 26, 1918) Fr. Decor-

40

sant referring to these losses gives an explanation on the supernatural plane which is not without interest. He writes:

"Since Easter, you have been awaiting a divine message which would enlighten and comfort both you and Cardinal Bourne in these dark and depressing days. Yesterday, Feast of St. Mark the Evangelist, Berthe Petit communicated to me the following message: 'My apostle Francis must dispel the pain and agony which he is enduring as a result of the hardships which have fallen upon the combatants of his country; this trial is necessary, for after My protection had enabled them to gain the victory, they attributed the glory of it to their own prowess. Reverses are now showing these soldiers how human means alone are powerless to repel the surge of invasion.' "

Early on the morning of Good Friday, March 29th, Jesus appeared to Berthe. He was covered with blood. He said to her: "If My voice had been fully heeded and My orders carried out, I would have put an end this very day to a struggle in which blood is being shed for the sake of an illusive victory. In the midst of so many victims I am reaping an abundant harvest of souls; the prolongation of the trial crushes the vain pride of a great many who were seeking nothing from life but pleasure or who were making their preparations for the persecution of My Church." And on the 1st of April: "The days to come will be terrible. There will be enormous losses. How strong and powerful the enemy still is will be plainly seen."

As events proved, immediately after their offensive of March 21st, the Germans began another in French Flanders, and yet another in West Flanders on April 9th. The English were driven back and lost all they had gained since May, 1917, and the Belgians, in the Mont Kemmel sector, suffered the fiercest and most perilous assaults. But on the 17th of April Ypres was saved and the enemy lost all hope of piercing the line to Calais.

Footnote to Chapter V:

Father Albert Condamin, S.J., was Professor of Sacred Scripture at the College, Ore Place, Hastings, and the author of articles in the "Revue Biblique." He was introduced to Fa-

41

ther Decorsant in 1910 by the Rev. Fr. Bainvel, S.J. When he recommended his soul to the prayers of Berthe Petit, Jesus said: "The soul of my servant Albert is very dear to Me."

In 1913, Jesus said again of him: "He is an untiring worker." And when told of this praise, the priest was astonished. Jesus said once more: "It is not because of the work of intelligence, or devotedness, or religious activity that I estimate in My divine mind either labor, or prayer, or renunciation. I perceive the motives that animate minds and hearts and my gaze rests there where I find true zeal for the good of souls, childlike humility and sincere renouncement. "Untiring" he is, therefore, who ceases not to seek Me in everything. This is what pleases My Heart. This is what attracts My glance of love."

The relations between Fr. Decorsant and Fr. Condamin having become very intimate, it was only natural that Berthe's director should turn to him, and this by Divine command, in the following terms: "Reverend and dear Father, the day before yesterday, Feast of the Seven Dolors, the Divine Master said to Berthe Petit: "The hour has come for My servant Albert who, as you know, is specially loved by My Heart and by that of My Mother, to aid in the work I have entrusted to you, by becoming the zealous apostle of the Sorrowful and Immaculate Heart of My Mother which has won for itself the gaze of My merciful Love. Blessings will follow the apostolate of my chosen servant, and every light will be given him for his co-operation. He will communicate the writings of your director to My apostle Francis ("the chief Bishop of England?", asked Berthe — "Yes," replied Jesus), whom I bless, and he will ardently plead before the Prelate the cause of the Sorrowful and Immaculate Heart of My Mother. Let My apostle Francis thus enlightened, adopt the devotion and promulgate it."

"Let him grant to the invocation "Sorrowful and Immaculate Heart of Mary, pray for us" the privilege it already has (100 days indulgence granted in 1911 by Cardinal Mercier). Let him propagate the devotion through the voice of his priests, so that souls may be duly prepared for the solemn consecration of their country to the Sorrowful and Immaculate Heart of My Mother. When he has fulfilled this, my apostle Francis will see My protection extended to his flock, his country and eventually the triumph of justice."

"As I have done in the case of your country and of France,

I offer to this nation the providential help of My merciful Heart."

Fr. Decorsant announced to Fr. Condamin the dispatch of documents which would enlighten him on his mission. Here is the reply: "I shall endeavor to do all I can to help you in your undertaking. If the work is truly of God and so dear to the Heart of Our Lord and of His Blessed Mother as the weighty documents amassed by you lead me to believe, why should I not be happy to co-operate? And if it be true that I am appointed for the special collaboration you speak of, I have good reason to be deeply affected while being filled with confusion at this honor."

Two weeks later, Fr. Condamin informed Fr. Decorsant that things were going very well, adding: "I sent everything on May 1st with a covering letter long enough to plead the cause, but not too long to cause fatigue."

On May 6th came the Cardinal's reply: "I have no need to tell you that I shall do all I can to fulfill the wishes of our Divine Master. The first free day, I shall go and see you at Hastings and we shall discuss the whole matter. I am most grateful for your letter, and I begged Our Lord through the intercession of His Blessed Mother to shower blessings on you."

To save the Prelate this journey, Fr. Condamin went to London. "His Eminence," he wrote, "welcomed me with great cordiality. He is entirely won over to your mission — convinced that there is no illusion, and he will act. This very day (the 24th) he is to mention the subject in a public sermon for an official consecration. He intends taking the first opportunity. But this will not be for two or three months; and you will find it very long. He hopes to issue a pastoral in which he will explain the matter, and specify the indulgences granted to the invocation."

"Our Reverend Father Rector who at first showed little enthusiasm for the subject that interests us, declared the other day that he was completely won over suddenly by reason of a vivid light he received on the admirable connection of these two ideas: extreme suffering united with absolute innocence in Mary — a thing which is very difficult to reconcile — the scandal of trial, or sufferings that we deem unmerited."

"I have decided," wrote Cardinal Bourne soon after to Father Condamin, "not to put off any longer what is so clearly the desire of our Divine Master. I have already preached on this subject, and used the invocation publicly, at Our Lady of Victories, Kensington, on May 24th."

Bookmarks bearing the invocation were, from this time, printed and propagated. And a pastoral letter from the Cardinal, on Trinity Sunday, June 18th, terminated thus: "Turn then with confidence to God, through the intercession and guidance of Her who in life-long anguish and incomparable compassion, has had the privilege, as no other creature, of sharing in the expiatory sacrifice of Her Divine Son. She has given Him everything that a creature could give, and He has bestowed upon Her gifts surpassing all those He has given to the rest of mankind. Ask of Her through the unparalleled sorrows of Her Sorrowful Heart, and Her stainless purity to show us how to profit by this heavy cross which God has allowed to fall upon the world — to unite all our sufferings, great and small with those of Jesus Crucified, and thus draw upon us, and upon the world the Peace of God which the world cannot give, and which can only be found in the complete acceptance of His Holy Will."

"We grant to all those who, in this mind, will devoutly say: 'Sorrowful and Immaculate Heart of Mary, pray for us' an indulgence of 200 days each time."

That same day, the Divine Master said to His servant: "The soul of My apostle has fully corresponded with My light, by welcoming this devotion, by drawing attention to it with all the fervor and active zeal which it deserves, and by preparatory prayer disposing hearts for the solemn consecration — source of salvation for souls and source of providential help which will ensure victory."

On Friday, June 30th, came the message: "On this Feast of My Heart, a twofold Feast in Heaven where reign our united Hearts, abundant blessings are being poured upon My apostle Francis, and upon all those who, thanks to this exhortation, are already invoking the Heart of My Mother in accordance with the formula which I have dictated. By a solemn consecration to the Sorrowful and Immaculate Heart of My Mother, he will soon deliver his country, the Church and the flock confided to him. I shall give ear to his pious aspirations. He will see, too, My divine intervention in all his anxieties. But I wish him to abandon all to Me with full confidence in the light which will guide him ever for the greater good and the triumph of My Church. My Mother, touched by this act of My apostle in honor of Her Heart, is giving him Her maternal protection, he will have the proof of this in the most consoling way when My Will is fully accomplished."

On July 25th, Fr. Condamin communicated the decision of the Cardinal to profit by the Feast of the Seven Dolors (Sept. 15th) to take the first step towards a solemn consecration.

Fr. Decorsant sent the following message from Our Lord on August 22nd to the English Prelate: "I ask My apostle Francis to exert an ever increasing activity in favor of the Sorrowful and Immaculate Heart of My Mother — an activity which will be reflected in the zealous preaching of His clergy, so that souls may turn in prayerful confidence to the Heart of My Mother. Soon My apostle will feel, personally, that the devotion will bring help in the hour of need, and eventual salvation to many souls."

"Let him hasten what he calls his 'first step' so that a still more solemn consecration may be timed for the Feast of the Dolors of My Mother — the great Feast of Her Heart as Co-Redemptrix."

"When the nation of My apostle Francis will be entirely dedicated to this Heart he will see that he has not listened to My word in vain, for My providential intervention is reserved for all the people consecrated to the Sorrowful and Immaculate Heart of My Mother. I wish thus to show the power of this Heart which is united in everything with My own."

"My apostle Francis will also see the increasing support of Benedict XV for this devotion to the Sorrows of the Heart of My Mother till the day when — the devotion having triumphed in the nations of My choice by reason of the zeal of their apostles — the glory of our united Hearts will extend everywhere for the salvation of souls."

On the 15th of August, the Cardinal consecrated England to the Heart of Mary, not however in a solemn manner. In the following month he was ill, and in answer to prayer for him, Our Lord replied: "It is I who dispose of life and death. I know the instruments that serve My purpose. You need not, therefore, be disturbed! You must abandon all to My leading. Let no illusion lead you to expect a human victory in the present struggle. The danger remains great for the nations drawn into this fight, and a happy issue can be obtained only through recourse, as I wish it, to the Sorrowful and Immaculate Heart of My Mother."

On December 24th, Berthe begged Our Lord that the Cardinal consecrate his country solemnly to the Heart of Mary on the following day (the communications were becoming even more difficult between Switzerland and England. Fr. Decorsant's correspondence was dispatched by diplomatic courier, but none the less, it often suffered long delay.) To this prayer, Jesus answered: "My apostle sees My intervention in the success of the combatants of his nation. He will carry out my wishes faithfully."

Actually, on the 8th of January, 1918, Fr. Decorsant received the following letter written on the 22nd of December by Fr. Condamin: "On the great Feast of Christmas will take place the solemn consecration. I received this morning the formula excellently printed and accompanied by a pressing letter which ordered the solemn recitation on Christmas Day — thereby dedicating anew to the loving care of the Sorrowful and Immaculate Heart of Mary, England and the vast Empire of which England is the parent and the home. It is recommended to make the act frequently: 200 days indulgence is granted to each recitation."

Following a further demand of Our Lord that the Cardinal once more consecrate his country, this time in thanksgiving, Fr. Decorsant wrote directly to Cardinal Bourne, April 30th in these terms: "To the consecration of his country to the Sorrowful and Immaculate Heart of My Mother, made by My apostle Francis, according to My orders, he owes My promised intervention from which has resulted the happy issue of the battle in favor of the defenders of his country."

"I should have intervened completely by a remarkable feat which would have led to the lasting peace I desired to give, a peace which would have assured the full victory of My Church, had the other nations acceded to My demand. The combatants have benefited by My protection plain to be seen by those who wish to open their eyes to the light and to acknowledge that it was impossible otherwise to have gained the victory over the enemy. My word has, therefore, been openly brought to pass: 'A chastisement will strike down the ambitious one on the soil invaded,' and that other word: 'I will break his might and his pride.' "

And when He had exposed in these terms the dangers that still menaced the world, the Divine Master continued thus: "The hurricane of calamity has not died down and grave dangers from within still threaten all the nations. For many amongst them there remains danger from without. My words will come to pass."

"To prevent these internal dangers in your country, Your Eminence, and to carry out the divine orders in their entirety, the Lord added: 'Let My apostle Francis know that My favorable gaze rests upon him, and his flock. Let him renew with the faithful the solemn consecration to the Sorrowful and Immaculate Heart of My Mother — this time in thanksgiving, for gratitude draws down still more favors. Let him confide to Me entirely his country and the Church of which he is the shepherd, in the way I shall inspire you. Thus will My reign be established firmly in that nation; then more and more souls will open their eyes to the truth; peace and prosperity will reign there, and My Mother, glorified in a fitting manner, will extend to them Her Maternal protection.' "

" 'Thus and in this way alone will the internal struggles die down. And I shall scatter blessings upon that nation. My apostle Francis will know the holy joys and consolations of the Shepherds who accomplish My Will.' "

CHAPTER VI

THE END OF THE FIRST WORLD WAR

MADAME PETIT, her daughter and Father Decorsant had left Lucerne by September, 1917. They were lodged at Fribourg in a section of Doctor Raymond's Clinic reserved for refugees during the War. It was staffed by Sisters of St. Thomas of Villanova, from Aix-en-Provence.

The travelers remained there until June, 1918. Doctor Raymond had organized Red Cross lectures for ambulance nurses, and Berthe followed these, obtaining her diploma with distinction. She excelled in making bandages and became a splendid nurse. Her time was divided between her mother, the sick and the prisoners of war whose letters she wrote, and to whom Father Decorsant gave spiritual help.

During his stay in Lucerne, the latter exercised his ministry in the boarding school of the Dominican Nuns who were occupying the Convent of the Dorothean Sisters expelled from Portugal, and also at the German Convent of the Sacred Heart exiled from France. The three exiles spent the months preceding the end of the war at Sarnen.

Already on the 6th of September, Jesus made the prophetic revelation which was to be verified only too well by the events which followed the Armistice: *"The leaders of this nation (Germany) who clearly see the peril of invasion with which their country is threatened, are preparing by tactics which no one suspects, and in full agreement with him whom I have pointed out to you as a scheming, hypocritical enemy of My Church, a plan which will temporarily save their nation. In consequence, she will not immediately receive the punishment she deserves."*

Nothing can be more evident than the fact that when Berthe Petit uttered these predictions, as coming from our Savior, neither she nor anyone else (except, of course, the high-ranking conspirators of the Masonic sect), was, humanly speaking, capable of foreseeing that these events would be speedily realized.

During the Holy Hour of October 16th, Our Lord sent the messenger whom He Himself had chosen in the 17th century to be the apostle of His Sacred Heart — Margaret Mary — to the servant of the Sorrowful and Immaculate Heart of Our Lady, to speak these consoling words:

"Peace be with you, for you are serving a cause so dear to the Sacred Heart. This Divine Heart deigned to turn to me during my earthly pilgrimage which ended without my seeing the glorification of the cause. This was for me a source of sorrow and agonizing suspense which gave me more tribulation than joy. You are fighting, you are suffering for the cause of the Blessed Virgin; and the immensity of the glory, which must flow from its triumph, now entails multiple obstacles which mean trials for your soul."

"But believe in a word which is beyond all doubt. Await its realization, in spite of darkness and anguish. Consider what has already been won for this cause, which the Eternal Son regards as His work of justice and love for His Mother. For you the hour is hard. It is one of struggle, but also of blind confidence which believes and takes for granted the liberty of the divine action in everything."

Turning away her gaze and looking afar, Margaret Mary ended her message saying:

"Poor France is in peril. She is inflated with pride and yet so many hardships will be hurled upon her before the day she is to rise again."

Jesus sealed these revelations by the following words on October 17th: "Had I not intervened in answer to recourse to the Sorrowful and Immaculate Heart of My Mother, and through the leading of My apostle Francis, victory would have been on the side of those, who long since had set all their energies to prepare and organize a vast scale war to attain their ambitious ends. Material strength would thus have prevailed over justice and right and this more especially so for your own country. For why should I come to the help of the people of a France intent on persecuting My Church, when the leaders should be earnestly organizing resistance to any invader. That is why trials will continue until the day when humbly acknowledging her errors, this nation will render Me My rights and give full liberty to My Church."

And on the 28th: "The world is hanging over the edge of the precipice. Confusion will reign increasingly and those who are now singing their victory will see it snatched out of their hands. My Justice does not preside over the intrigues of those who are working in their own interests towards a peace which does not merit the name, and which can never be genuine except through My intervention."

On the 11th of November, the Armistice was signed and the invader was punished "on the soil unjustly invaded." Referring to this, "Le Matin" made a significant remark: "During the few days that were to lead to the magnificent triumph of our army — which we would have been justified in expecting — we were actually on the verge of agreeing amongst ourselves to suspend hostilities . . . "

Berthe Petit and Abbé Decorsant at Louvignies

Jesus said to Berthe: "I have permitted everything, because My wishes for the Heart of My Mother have not been fulfilled . . ."

And indeed, according to His prediction made ten months before and transmitted to Cardinal Bourne who had obeyed His Will, the war ended "abruptly, rapidly, gloriously" in favor of the English who alone realized their war aims.

As a result of a reiterated divine command expressed to Berthe Petit and destined for the Archbishop of Westminster, the latter again consecrated his country to the Sorrowful and Immaculate Heart, in thanksgiving and in accordance with an appropriate formula revealed once again to the servant of God. The ceremony took place with great solemnity on May 24, 1919. In a letter on this subject to Father Decorsant, the Cardinal prayed that Our Lord bless abundantly his correspondent "and also your spiritual child whom He has chosen to be the instrument of His bounty."

At the beginning of the winter of 1918, Madame Petit and Berthe together with Father Decorsant remained for one year at Vevey, at the Villa Antonia, a Guest-House kept by Madame Taneron (Sr. Joseph of the Sacred Heart), Superior of the Trinitarian Sisters of Valence (France) at this time exiled in Switzerland.

Berthe left an unforgettable memory there and she remained in constant touch with Madame Taneron as well as Sr. Valesine and Sr. Marie Florentine B. Of these, the two first mentioned are dead and the Villa Antonia has been demolished.

In July, 1919, the Divine Master spoke as follows to Berthe: "Internal strife is more rampant than ever in your country. It is being fanned by the evil seed sown by the invader; it is fed by egoism, pride and jealousy — malevolent germs which can only generate moral ruin. I continue to have pity on a country which defended its honor at the cost of the greatest sacrifices, and on a sovereign faithful to his duty. To save this nation, I have wished, and continue to wish, that it should be solemnly consecrated to the Heart of My Mother. People must know that they are consecrated to Her Sorrowful and Immaculate Heart, to the end that they may invoke this Heart; so that in time of danger it may be obvious to all that I have intervened because of this consecration and that My Mother is worthy to be thanked and glorified for ever."

"Time will prove that peace established without Me and without him [7] who speaks in My Name, has no stability. The nation which is considered to be vanquished, but whose forces are only momentarily diminished, will remain a menace for your country, and likewise for France. Confusion and terror will steadily spread through every nation."

"Because this peace is not Mine, wars will be rekindled on every side — civil war and racial war. What would have been so noble, so true, so beautiful, so lasting in its fulfillment is consequently delayed . . ."

"Humanity is advancing towards a frightful scourge which will divide the nations more and more; it will reduce human schemes to nothingness; it will break the pride of the powers

---

[7] The reference is to the Holy Father: For the establishment of a just and lasting peace in 1919, Benedict XV was not consulted any more than was Pius XII in 1945.

that be; it will show that nothing subsists without Me and that I remain the only Master of the destinies of nations." Jesus also deigned to enlighten His servant on the wording of the consecration for the "*post-war*" period. We give it in the form in which it has been spread all over the world:

TEXT OF THE CONSECRATION TO THE SORROWFUL AND IMMACULATE HEART OF MARY

Lord Jesus, King of kings, many of us never ceased to place full confidence in Your Divine Heart during the long trial of war. Many, likewise, have implored the help of Your Mother, and we wish to show our gratitude by consecrating ourselves to Her Sorrowful and Immaculate Heart.

It is fitting that we should honor this Sorrowful Heart by special veneration. For Your Mother, O Lord, acquired this title when She shared Your Passion and thus co-operated in the work of our Redemption; a just title which we believe to be dear to Your Heart, and to Her Heart pierced with the wound of Yours.

We, therefore, O Blessed Mother, consecrate to Your Sorrowful and Immaculate Heart, our persons, our families and our country. We beseech You to come to our help as a Mother.

Behold the trials that oppress us, the menace of evil and the dangers that surround us. We beseech You to obtain for us from Your Divine Son, solace in suffering, social unity between classes and the preservation of peace.

May the reign of the Sacred Heart, a reign of justice and love, be extended throughout our dear country, and may Your Sorrowful and Immaculate Heart, loved and invoked, reign over us also, O Blessed Mother, and ever obtain for us the mercy and blessing of God.

CHAPTER VII

RETURN TO BELGIUM: MOURNFUL PREDICTIONS

IN OCTOBER, 1919, Berthe and her mother left Switzerland and returned to Brussels after an absence of five years. To their dismay, they found that their beloved home in the Rue du Cornet had been completely ruined and plundered during the German occupation. The Divine Master had not spared them this trial which completely upset their lives once more.

They sought hospitality from the Sisters of the Sacred Heart at Overyssche and it was here, on March 26, 1922, that Madame Petit died at the age of 86. She was surrounded by the most attentive care and tender affection of her daughter and of Father Decorsant whom she regarded as her son.

Immediately on her return to Belgium, Berthe Petit had an interview with Cardinal Mercier. His Eminence, while remaining in contact with her, judged it wise in view of his numerous pastoral occupations, to confide her for closer spiritual direction to his friend Msgr. Piéraerts, Chaplain to the Court. Their first meeting took place on January 21, 1920.

"Msgr. Piéraerts," wrote Berthe, "spoke to me of the Devotion as most dear to him." From that moment, and until the death of the venerable Prelate (May, 1926) an intimate spiritual relationship was established between him and Berthe whom he always spoke of as "the saint." Here is one example of his exceedingly paternal letters to her. It is dated 14th of January, 1922.

"MY DEAR CHILD,
You know the place you have in my prayer, and the intimate association of my whole soul with your pious and apostolic desire to aspire for the glory of the Sorrowful and Immaculate Heart of Mary. Knowing this, be assured of all my wishes, which I beg you to share with your holy director and with your good mother."

Cardinal Granito di Belmonte also remained in continual paternal correspondence with her and with Fr. Decorsant. In March, 1921, he served as intermediary to present to the Holy

Father a report of all that had been done in regard to the Devotion during the previous four years, the steps taken — though without apparent result; the prophecies, some of which were already verified and others were to follow in due course. One of these was most impressive: "The ravening nation desirous of a prompt revenge is preparing a destructive mechanism which will soon be ready. Then, rapidly and with her thorough organization she will swoop down upon those whom she would lay low."

The report also gave the revelations of Our Lord, dated October, 1920, when the Savior exalted the merits of the Sorrows of His Mother in these terms: "The title of Immaculate belongs to the whole being of My Mother and not specially to Her Heart. This title flows from my gratuitous gift to the Virgin who was to give me birth. My Mother has acquired for her Heart the title of Sorrowful by sharing generously in all the sufferings of My Heart and My Body from the crib to the cross. There is not one of these Sorrows which did not pierce the Heart of My Mother. Living image of My crucified Body, her virginal flesh bore the invisible marks of My wounds as her Heart felt the Sorrows of My own. Nothing could ever tarnish the incorruptibility of her Immaculate Heart."

"The title of 'Sorrowful' belongs therefore to the Heart of My Mother, and more than any other, this title is dear to Her because it springs from the union of her Heart with Mine in the redemption of humanity. This title has been acquired by her through her full participation in My Calvary, and it precedes the gratuitous title 'Immaculate' which My love bestowed upon her by a singular privilege."

On June 21, 1921, the Divine Master uttered the following words, the realization of which no one could then foresee: "Events are unleashed in Italy. Their work of destruction is but a feeble image of the punishment which will strike this nation, which is to be deceived in the evil day by motives cleverly veiled." And on another day: "When he of whom I have spoken to you will be struck down, the cataclysm will be at hand."

On October 24th of that same year, it was Our Lady who spoke thus: "Events are nearing, like an ever growing shadow imperceptibly widening, and all the while concealing frightful sparks which will plunge the nations once again into fire and blood. Oh! What a terrifying thought! My maternal Heart would be broken, did I not know that divine Justice is intervening for the salvation of souls and the cleansing of nations . . ."

These words are fully in accord with those pronounced in 1846 by the Sorrowful Virgin to the shepherds of La Salette; and more recently, in 1917, to the shepherd children of Fatima, and later, in 1932, to the children at Beauraing by the Blessed Virgin of the Rosary.

In January, 1922, His Holiness, Benedict XV, died rather suddenly and Pius XI ascended the Throne of Peter.

On February 6th, Our Lord said: "My apostle will arise at the appointed hour when the horrible cataclysm, which is coming, will have overthrown the machinations of men and their deplorable state-craft. It is not at the present time that My wish concerning the glory of My Mother will be accomplished. A period of waiting is still necessary for the work to grow in greatness."

On the 29th of September, Father Decorsant transmitted to Cardinal Granito di Belmonte the following message which Our Lady gave to his spiritual child: "My daughter, let your souls bless my Son for the choice He has made of you in the accomplishment of His express wish. Events have occurred, preparations are made which are the unassailable foundations for the cause which you serve. The work will attain its end and this with the amplitude willed by God. The way which leads to this result is arid, devoid of repose, at times even painful for your souls, as you labor to comply with my requests. But have confidence: strife will come to an end and my Son will triumph. See how humanity is crushed by sorrow, while evil is diabolically making progress. There have been catastrophes; there will be more. But what are they? Merely a beginning, a feeble image of the dreadful calamities predicted to you by my Son!. . ."

"Persevere in your task by complete forgetfulness of yourselves, and by the one only thought of obeying my Son for the realization of His designs. My Heart, full of pity for humanity, bows down before divine Justice which is on the way to manifesting itself on a magnificent scale. Each nation is preparing its own punishment: some are actuated by their rapacity, others by their ambitions, while others again refuse to put an end to the ravages of passion. As for you, our servants, look with confidence to a future guided by infinite Wisdom, Mercy and Power."

Although promises were made with regard to the magnificent development of the Devotion to the Sorrowful and Immaculate Heart of Mary, and encouragement given to the servant of God and to her priest, it was quite obviously never guaranteed that they would live to witness this transformation of the world! Is it not the vocation of apostles to live in sacrifices? They are sowers: others will reap the harvest.

On October 12, 1923, Cardinal Granito confided to Father Decorsant the fact of his miraculous cure. It was obtained, thanks to the intercession of her who was at that time "Blessed Teresa of the Child Jesus."

He added in his Italianized French:

"See now, Father what your prayers have obtained without your suspecting it!... Now, I would ask you and Berthe Petit to beg from Jesus and the Blessed Virgin Mary, the grace that I may save my soul and that I may show myself grateful for all the favors and mercies I am receiving. I bless you and your spiritual daughter, and I thank you for the charity of the holy prayers you are offering for me."

CHAPTER VIII

THE ASCENT TO CALVARY

IN October, 1923, Berthe, who since her mother's death was living with friends, had a very bad accident. She fell against a piece of furniture, which had been moved out of its usual place, and nearly broke her breastbone. She remained for a long time in a stooped position. Two days after this fall, the Divine Master said to her during thanksgiving: "Your trial is painful to your customary activity. It could have happened to others, but I choose my victims according to the amount of suffering they are willing to accept and to their complete abandonment, leaving Me free to use it as I desire. The trial is meritorious in the measure in which it is hard and crucifying to nature. It can neither surprise nor discourage those who know that I am the supreme Master!"

On the 20th, Our Lady came in her turn: "Your trial would have had fatal consequences if it had not been expressly permitted. You are broken and bruised; there will remain painful scars, but I shall cure you when the amount of suffering needed by my Divine Son will be attained. I am leaving succor which will help you bear your pain."

On the 24th, during Holy Hour, Berthe suddenly felt an internal shock on the wounded spot in the sternum which she had been bathing every day with Lourdes water, and then Our Lady appeared to her saying: "I shall complete your cure, but I am leaving the marks of your fall which, humanly speaking, would have been fatal. You require strength to continue the great task indicated by my Son, Who is prolonging your life in accordance with His designs."

The year 1924 began for the patient with a heart attack which the Blessed Virgin came to relieve and to cure as She had already done.

In a letter of February 11th, addressed to Cardinal Granito, Father Decorsant quoted the following words of Our Lord to His servant in response to her humble request concerning Italy and its Duce — words which today have an aspect of impressive reality. They completed and confirmed the revelations of June, 1921:

"Those who allow themselves to be dominated by pride and who are guided by ambition, will not escape My justice. The present government of that nation is motivated by its passions. That government which has the semblance of giving promise of a better era, will collapse in disillusionment. The man you have named is veiling his ambition under the guise of benevolence to the Church. This is but one more ruse planned by the ungodly sect to attain the end towards which its efforts are directed, by lulling to sleep all uneasiness."

Saint Joseph appeared several times to the servant of God, notably on March 19, 1924, with the object of encouraging the Cardinal to devote himself to the Devotion dear to the Mother of God. New revelations were communicated to her on September 24, 1924: "All the nations are heading towards a frightful cataclysm. I alone can appease the hatred and the discord, and hasten the reign of peace. I shall do it when My wishes for the Heart of My Mother will be accomplished. It will come to pass when the hour of despair will strike — an hour towards which everything is moving. Then, in response to the supplications which will ascend to the Sorrowful and Immaculate Heart of My Mother, I will manifest My power by a miraculous intervention which will impress everyone. The whole of Christendom will bow before this triumph which I, as Son, have determined for My Mother. Tell My apostle that this Sorrowful Heart must be more and more his dwelling."

In October, 1925, the Jubilee Year, Berthe, her sister and a friend accompanied by Father Decorsant left for Rome where once again they saw Cardinal Granito di Belmonte who received them cordially, coming himself to the Via Sistina to welcome them.

His Eminence announced his visit in the following terms: "Dear Father, Saturday morning, about 10 o'clock I shall be with you. I bless you and I bless Mlle. Petit. Pray for me."

Next morning, Feast of All Saints, Father Decorsant and his spiritual daughter went to the church of the Capuchin Fathers where the Cardinal was consecrating a bishop. At the close of the ceremony, they received his blessing with his paternal smile and a pleasant word.

In another interview, this time with Father Decorsant alone, His Eminence handed him his photograph with this dedication, in his own handwriting: "To Mademoiselle Petit, the child of the Sorrowful Heart of Mary, Mother of God."

Berthe Petit (in the center) Abbé Decorsant and friends in the garden of the Villa des Deux Alice

Thanking Cardinal Granito, Berthe wrote: —

"YOUR EMINENCE,
   With filial emotion and profound gratitude I have received the large and beautiful photograph which you have autographed and which the child of the Sorrowful and Immaculate Heart of Mary will never look upon without begging the Mother of God to grant your Paternity all the graces you may desire."

On November 7th, the travelers were admitted to a semi-private audience with His Holiness Pius XI, and in the afternoon of the same day, Berthe and Father Decorsant had a long conversation with Cardinal Granito in his own apartment.

Their stay in Rome came to an end on November 12th, but without any steps having been taken to further the Devotion.

We are prompted to ask why? The answer is that the Divine Master had not manifested His Will in this regard, and His servant, in the course of her mission never acted on her own initiative.

At this time, the glorious career of Cardinal Mercier was drawing to a close. The life of the former and well-beloved Director of St. Louis College, Monsignor Piéraerts, Chaplain at the Royal Court was likewise coming to an end. Berthe Petit was informed of all this by revelation already on December 8th, and she felt deep sorrow at the thought of losing both her most precious supporters.

On January 4th, on his way to the nursing home in the Rue des Cendres, Cardinal Mercier called on his friend, who likewise was very ill at the Rue Rogier where Berthe Petit happened to be visiting.

It was a last and touching interview! On the 23rd, His Eminence died.

On this occasion, Fr. Decorsant received (January 30th) the following letter from Cardinal Granito:

"DEAR FATHER,
    I am already in arrears with my thanks, but not at all with my poor prayers as there is always a share in them for you and Mlle. Petit. My thoughts have been very much with you these days, on account of the death of the great Cardinal Mercier! Mlle. found in him a strong support and protection! She will feel this loss! It is not without reason that she has taken Our Lady of Sorrows as her model! I bless you and to Mademoiselle I send my very special benediction!"

On May 26th, the Court Chaplain died.

The following year, Berthe found in Bishop Legraive, the auxiliary bishop, a director and, at the same time, a real Father. This was balm for her bruised soul.

During the summer of 1926, Berthe went on a journey to Colmar and on a pilgrimage to "Trois Epis." In 1927, she went to Wattweiler, to stay with a friend whom she had known in Switzerland.

A great change occurred in Berthe's life during 1927. The training school for the Nurses of St. Camille which owned the Institute of the "Deux Alice" at Uccle, had an empty house at its garden gate. It had previously served as a chaplain's residence and the tenancy was now offered to Berthe who took possession of it in October.

The Château de Louvignies, front view

The "Villa of the Deux Alice" soon became an oasis, which only privileged persons were allowed to enter. No one ever left it without having experienced the most exquisite hospitality and supreme consolation, derived from the supernatural strength of her who, notwithstanding all her sufferings, was so selfless and devoted.

The private oratory, which was her privilege for several years, was re-established at the Villa. The tiny chapel was close to her room. The Sacred Host irradiated beams of light in this dwelling of His choice. Who would dare to penetrate the secret of those nights when the "apostle," deprived of sleep, overwhelmed with pain, and devoured by thirst, held her mysterious and inexpressible colloquy with Him Who alone was her life!

At this time the management of the "Deux Alice" was transferred to the Sisters of Good Hope of Binche. They often appealed to Fr. Decorsant to exercise his sacred ministry for the benefit of the patients of the Institute.

In 1928, Berthe, accompanied by Fr. Decorsant, went for the first time to stay at the Castle of Louvignies where from now to the end of her life she was to go every year during the summer months. For the family there, and for all their staff, her stay was an unforgettable memory and a source of grace.

If the fresh country air and the complete rest restored the poor invalid somewhat, trials, none the less, continued to assail her there. One day she missed her footing at the top of the six steps leading to the cemetery and she was violently thrown headforemost. Was it the devil, as at Lucerne? She had just pleaded ardently for a soul in peril! . . . Anyone else would have been shattered to pieces. She was severely bruised, but this time there were no grievous consequences of her fall. There were other times, when her knees would suddenly become dislocated causing her excruciating pain.

The six years that follow (1928-1934) were characterized by a diversity of sufferings which were steadily intensified, but which did not hinder the activity of the servant of God. She suffered congestion of the liver, and then of the kidneys; the dorsal vertebrae disclosed, as revealed by X-ray, characteristic and formidable deformations commonly called "parrot beaks"; her falls became more frequent; intolerable pains seized the middle finger of her right hand, which had been poisoned by the prick of a cactus.

The Divine Master was molding this soul. Our Lady appeared to her (December 29, 1930) and promised her "nothing but suffering!" On Good Friday of the following year, Berthe had to endure sufferings greater than ever before. That night, her lips and tongue were cleft and bled profusely. The wound in her side likewise opened. The palms of her hands and feet caused her excruciating pain without, however, opening. She begged Jesus that she might be able to hide from everyone the marks He deigned to send her. "The world is inundated with crime, and there are the sins of priests, and the scandal of immodest fashions. The evils that will break upon the world will be frightful." During the night of February 10, 1932, the Blessed Virgin came to her. The room was filled for a long time with the most exquisite fragrance and the air resounded with the strains of ravishing music. Three times did the Virgin-Mother place her hand on Berthe's forehead saying: "What suffering! What suffering! What suffering!"

Monsignor Piéraerts appeared to her on the anniversary of his death (May 26, 1932), and said: "Be at peace, the work will be fully accomplished. In Heaven I see its vast extent, and all its consequences."

Jesus said (November, 1932): "You are like Me, courageous on your cross, but it is I who give you strength. It is a time of suffering — determined by Me, uncertain for you." At this time, Berthe's constant prayer was: "Let nothing, O Lord, remain fruitless in my day."

The year 1934 was a most painful one. In May, acute arthritis of both feet made walking impossible. In October, there appeared a large abcess on her neck together with a condition of general poisoning. Surgical treatment was deemed necessary. Lourdes water was applied. On the morning the operation was to take place, the abcess burst of itself, to the great surprise of the surgeon, so that surgery was not needed.

Ever valiant, in spite of all, the poor victim was devoted to everyone, to the sick who were recommended to her at the nursing home, but above all to her chaplain, whose health was deteriorating more and more: Father Decorsant could now celebrate Holy Mass but rarely. Henceforward, not to miss her daily Mass, Berthe had to cross the snow-covered garden, very painfully to the chapel of the Institute.

On April 27th, at the close of the Jubilee Year at Lourdes, Our Lord told her: "The storm is abating. So many prayers are ascending to me! So many supplications, sincere and ardent, are being sent up to My Heart and through that of My Mother, that I will impose on the mighty one an era of peace, of short duration however, because the spirit of evil does not cease to incite and to goad the pride of any nation which lives only on the thought of revenge and domination."

The first day of December, Jesus called to Himself that faithful servant of His, the "chosen priest" who had offered himself to God at the very moment of the sacrifice made by a predestined soul in the chapel of the Capuchin Fathers at Enghien. The French Abbé had received the delicate mission to watch over this favored child and after the death of her parents had to provide, during her illnesses, that she might have the happiness of the Holy Sacrifice of the Mass and the sustenance of her heavenly food. He had to share in her life's work, and to receive and transmit the messages of the Divine Master. He was, above all, a priestly soul, a generous apostolic soul, one who, having heard the command of God, left everything in order to dedicate himself to the glory of the Mother of the Savior. Neither he nor his spiritual daughter had the supreme consolation of seeing the aim of their lives realized! His "fiat" was all the more noble and meritorious!

Six years previous, in 1928, Fr. Decorsant had been called upon to transmit a solemn warning which concluded thus: "If men could see the frightful means of destruction and if they would reflect on what is being prepared for a future war of revenge, there is no one who would not wish to die! Belgium, dangerously menaced, is more in peril than she realizes: she will be saved neither by her prudence, nor by her strength. She will not secure any triumph against her enemies. She can defend herself only with help from Heaven. She has no other refuge than the arms of God. He will open His divine arms at the prayer of His Mother, the Virgin Mary, and on condition that this Kingdom be consecrated to the Sorrowful and Immaculate Heart of the Mother of God and of men."

Worn out as she was by emotion and fatigue on the death of the "good Father," Berthe asked the Dorothean Sisters whom she had formerly known at Lucerne to give her hospitality during the Christmas festivities. She spent more than a fortnight in retreat at their house, in the Rue Jordaens, and then returned to her former abode. Here she shared her solitude with a friend who, for more than forty years, had been most devoted to her. They were never again to be separated. The chaplain of the nursing home brought Berthe Holy Communion every morning, as it had become impossible for her to walk to the chapel of the Institute.

In February she resigned herself to have an operation on one of her fingers which was infected with "tophus," a species of growth on the articulations. It proved to be an extremely painful operation, the result of which was futile and even unfortunate. Not only did the middle finger remain incurable, but all the other fingers in turn absorbed the uratoma as it forced its way through the tissues. The application of ultra violet rays and other remedies all equally failed.

Of all the physical sufferings which Berthe endured, this was one of the most painful and depressing for her very active nature. Indeed the extensive correspondence she had with all the souls in distress who came to her for comfort or advice, became more and more difficult and occasioned her ever greater suffering. Nevertheless, she undertook this work with marvelous courage, holding the pen, which soon had to give place to pencil, between her poor shriveled fingers.

She was an expert at needlework and crocheting. How many friends, young mothers, received lovely woollies, baby coats, scarves and shawls at which Berthe excelled in the make-up and in the tasteful blend of color. To her very last days she forced her poor fingers to work, but at what a price of suffering! . . .

Berthe was a first-rate cook. She was most successful in training others in the culinary art. She had taken lessons from a chef and though she herself took no nourishment, she did her utmost to ensure that all meals should be very thoroughly prepared. But the heat of the oven was exceedingly trying and even the smell of food most repugnant to her. You could not do her a greater favor than to appreciate the dainties she had purchased or made herself. Her one desire was always to give pleasure to others.

A long sojourn at Louvignies in July-August, 1936, restored her strength somewhat, but only on the condition that she refrained from any early morning walks to the village church. Every day, the parish priest brought her the Blessed Sacrament. She received Holy Communion in bed with the most profound recollection. It was then especially that one could feel how much Jesus was her life. As soon as she had absorbed the Sacred Host, she would remain motionless as a statue, her head on the pillow, her eyes closed and her hands joined. You could touch her, or speak to her, but she perceived nothing for she was no longer of this world. God was conversing with her, and she with Him. Sometimes a tear would fall from her eyes and her countenance would take on an expression of sorrow; then, suddenly, her sweet face would light up and a delightful smile play on her lips.

The condition usually lasted about three quarters of an hour. Little by little she would regain contact with the world, first by vocal prayer as one could see in the movement of her lips, then by the suffering which, as soon as consciousness returned, gripped her again and asserted its rights. She sometimes admitted how very hard it was to feel that the Real Presence was leaving her, to give place to the sad realities of life. One could have wished to withdraw to leave her longer to the supernatural, but this she would not allow, for she was bent on taking up whatever duty awaited her. This taking possession of her by God did not come about in an intermittent way; it occurred every day, and for many years, without exception.

**Berthe Petit's drawing room in
Uccle, Rue Joseph Stallaert**

In 1937, the servant of God was again at Lourdes. She went there to obtain, not a cure, but an alleviation of her sufferings, so that she might resume her activities in some measure. Actually, her sufferings increased the more during her stay.

Indeed, two days after her arrival in the company of her friend, she was assailed by a violent attack of gout on both feet which became extremely swollen, causing her darts of pain. To go to the Grotto was now out of the question! Neither was a pilgrimage possible. She had to leave the hotel and seek admittance at St. Bernadette's Hospital, kept by the Sisters of Nevers. Here she was obliged to remain a whole month for treatment.

She was always in spirit at the Sanctuary, whence came

the soft murmur of the pilgrim chant, and she languished at not being able to spend long hours of ecstasy at the Grotto. The Sisters, especially the Superior who had quickly sensed an exceptional soul in the person of their patient, endeavored in a thousand delicate ways, to ease her martyrdom. Towards the end of her stay, they took her several times in an invalid chair to Our Lady of the Grotto.

Berthe left Lourdes with, no doubt, an abundant harvest of souls. But Mary had given her to understand once more that, as a lover of the Sorrowful Heart, she was to expect thorns, and very few roses . . . A fresh trial awaited her on her return home. The Community of the Sisters of Charity of Ghent, who had taken up the direction of the nursing home of the "Deux Alice," had lately purchased the Institute and had claimed the "Villa" as a residence for their Chaplain. Berthe had to leave the place she loved, after a sojourn of ten years, which she declared were the happiest of her life. The change was heartbreaking and it was all the more distressing because from now on she could no longer be in such close proximity to the Blessed Sacrament.

At Berthe's new abode, the flat which she shared with her faithful friend Mademoiselle L. F. at Rue Joseph Stallaert, (Uccle), a hearty welcome was extended to everyone. Her sister, her numerous nephews and nieces, her intimate friends, souls in distress who were sent to her, members of the clergy, nuns — all came in turn to seek counsel, light, and spiritual renewal. No one ever went away disappointed. Of her sufferings she spoke little, but how much she shared those of others! . . . And despite this, she believed herself from this time forward to be inferior to her task! The Divine Master was chiseling, carving the raw flesh of her soul, that soul whose moral sufferings were far greater than her incredible physical pains.

The winter of 1937 was difficult for her on account of her early morning outings to the Church of the Annunciation, her parish. And in the month of March, 1938, she was attacked by acute rheumatism in her hands and feet. Henceforward, the Procurator of the *Péres des Missions Africaines,* Father Kn. . . agreed to bring her Holy Communion daily. In the course of that month, the Blessed Virgin came to her one night of frightful suffering, and said: "All for my Son! Do not refuse human aid and comfort, your sufferings are beyond human endurance. But I am near you — the Mother who is watching over all your pains which are so pleasing to my Son. Give thanks to God Who has accepted your offering, and taken it for the sanctification of your soul — for that of the clergy, and for the peace of the sad world." Saying this, two big tears fell from the eyes of Our Lady.

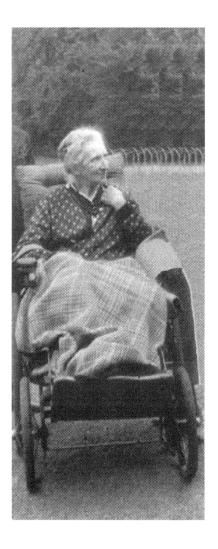

Berthe Petit at Louvignies (1939)

During her month's stay at Louvignies, her sufferings never ceased. At the end of August, in the hope of acquiring new strength in the buoyant air of Switzerland, she spent a month at Sarnten. The weather was disastrous — nothing but squalls and storms. In consequence came the return of those cruel darting pains.

On September 24th, she returned to Belgium, precisely when the first rumors of the War were spreading. On the 26th, 27th, and 28th there took place what was styled "Mobilization for Peace." The situation was alarming. Berthe alone remained calm. She contented herself by saying: "It will break out . . . but later on." On the 29th, the Munich Conference brought a respite. On the 30th, the King ordered demobilization.

Since the New Year 1939, the state of Berthe's health was steadily growing worse. Her sufferings became well-nigh unbearable. At length her friends persuaded her to seek medical advice. The new expedient was no improvement over the former; the treatment was ineffective — even harmful. Her stomach rejected all remedies, and a course of anti-rheumatic injections, far from effecting a cure, brought about a relapse of arthritis to her feet as soon as she arrived at Louvignies. The greater part of her stay there was spent in bed, her sufferings always on the increase.

"Remain in peace, you are one of my crucified members," Jesus said to her.

Bishop Legraive, always so paternal towards her, wrote as follows (August 8th) in reply to a letter from the Countess A. de V. on the state of the patient's health:

> "I thank you for having given me news about Mlle. Petit. I sympathize with the sorrowful trial of this martyr, so beloved by Our Lord Who, as a proof of His predilection, keeps her visibly on the arms of His cross. There is no doubt that the angelic resignation of this soul draws down choicest blessings on all those whom she wishes to benefit by her merits. May I beg of you to inform me of Mlle.'s return to Brussels? I shall deem it a privilege to visit her."
>
> "Meanwhile, be good enough to assure her of my constant memento at the altar. I promise that I will associate your name with that of her who is so worthy of our profound veneration."

CHAPTER IX

THE GREAT TRIAL

Tribulation was again to visit the poor victim on September 29, 1939 — a forerunner of the tragic events of 1940. One afternoon, in her flat at the Rue Joseph Stallaert, when she was doing her correspondence, Berthe stood up to go to her bedroom. Suddenly she fell forward, the result no doubt of a heart attack. Her right leg was doubled under her and the pain was atrocious. An X-ray revealed fracture of the neck of the femur and the patient was condemned to six week's absolute immobility. The surgeon did not hide the fact that the case, in view of the weakness of the subject, combined with her lack of nourishment, was now well nigh hopeless.

Towards the end of October, there was an embolism, which was followed by paralysis of the left hand. This time the doctor held no further hope. . . . But the gracious Virgin Mother was there watching: "Your Calvary is not over," she said; "if you did but know how eagerly my Son is gathering your sufferings for the salvation of souls and for the alleviation of the present calamities, not one of them would crush you without being a joy."

To those around her, Berthe said with a yearning smile: "I am worn out with suffering, and yet, happy to suffer; because suffering, unlike joy, leaves no void."

The convalescence was extremely long and depressing, especially for a nature like hers. Owing to lack of nourishment, "callus" (the bone material formed in process of the healing of bone fracture) showed no sign of development. Her leg was shortened by two centimeters and when walking was again possible, it was — and remained — most painful.

The political horizon, meanwhile, became darker as the days wore on and Berthe did not seek to conceal the gravity of events. She trembled for her own country, although she knew that any invader would be chastised. Had not Our Lord said on September 1st: "That nation is on the way to its own undoing. It is responsible for its illusory pride."

On January 22, 1940, the following words rang in her ears like a death-knell: "Belgium will be invaded."

The horrible reality was to be confirmed in April. "The rapidity of events will take people by surprise," she said. "It will be the ruin of our country." [8]

Indeed, on Friday, May 10th, the die was cast for Belgium. . . .

Calm in the presence of the general turmoil, the servant of God always tried to hold back those who thought to find safety in flight, and to reiterate once more the remedy for the agony of the moment. Our Lord insisted thus on July 2nd: "It is hearts that must be changed. This will be accomplished only by the Devotion proclaimed, explained, preached and recommended everywhere. Recourse to My Mother under the title I wish for her universally, *is the last help I shall give before the end of time.*"

A new trial, a moral one this time, lacerated the soul of Berthe. Her venerated director, Bishop Legraive, who had been ailing during the previous year, was taken from her on June 10th. She carefully kept his last letter, dated April 29th:

"Your friend has told me of your cruel sufferings which keep you more than ever on the cross of your Divine Spouse. She has given me the assurance that Holy Communion is being brought to you every day. It is your only nourishment and how very necessary!"

"I have just read in the Office of St. Catherine of Siena, whose feast it will be tomorrow, that she sometimes fasted from Ash Wednesday till the Ascension. But you, my poor child, fast all the year round and for how many years! St. Catherine suffered very much and died at the age of 33. Is it possible that her physical sufferings equaled yours? If the good God prolongs your existence and your long martyrdom, the reason must be that, through your sufferings, He harvests souls for His Paradise!"

"Courage, dear child, you are sowing in tears, you will reap in joy. I am giving you my blessing."

In spite of events, Berthe was able to go to Louvignies for her usual sojourn during the summer of 1941. She was in a very weak condition, but she had lost none of her hold on souls. Just the contrary. . . . In a wheelchair she had the con-

---

[8] The word "ruin" was not too strong for Belgium was obliged to adopt a new coinage after her liberation.

solation of being able to visit the Blessed Sacrament in the little church of the village; once more to visit the sick who gained courage at her visit, and to interest herself in the little children to whom she distributed many good things. They were ever on the look out for her arrival and her smile gained all hearts.

On her return to Brussels it was a joy for her, as well as a sweet consolation, to be honored by a visit of Her Majesty Queen Elisabeth of the Belgians.

She was also visited by Countess Gh. de C., lady-in-waiting, who, recalling these hours, wrote as follows on December 12, 1943: —

> "I became acquainted with Berthe Petit in 1927, after the death of Monsignor Piéraerts (chaplain to the Royal Court). Being very friendly with him, I often begged his prayers and he said to me on one occasion: "I shall confide your request to a very holy soul to whom Cardinal Mercier sometimes has recourse to obtain graces." But Monsignor Piéraerts never told me her name. Soon after his death, a mutual friend brought Berthe to visit me. The thought struck me: It is Monsignor Piéraerts who sent her to me!"
>
> "Her beautiful eyes, so clear, so full of faith, seemed to see what we could not. What was remarkable in her, was that her physical trials, her terrible sufferings never altered the clearness of her thought or the balance of her judgment. Descending from the heights of contemplation to bend down with sympathy over human miseries she was able to give practical advice to her friends — even in temporal matters."

In the midst of the turmoil, Berthe was anxious to restore calm and confidence to those around her and she obtained the following assurance from Her Divine Master on November 4, 1941: "The invader is at My Mercy for the punishment he deserves. Justice will be done in everything. The chastisement is rumbling, the leaders feel it coming near, they dread it and they realize that they can do nothing to avert it. It is then that My judgment and the power of My Will shall be made known. My Work will never fall short of achievement. Belgium will again be prosperous."

And on December 8th: "The safety of your country, internal peace and confidence in My Church will revive through the spread of the Devotion and the Consecration which I wish in order that the Sorrowful and Immaculate Heart of My Mother, united in all to My Heart, may be loved and glorified. Deliverance will thus be the work of our two Hearts, the triumph of our love for the people upon whom this Consecration will bestow confidence according to My promises."

And on one of the days following came another assurance: "By confident consecration to My Mother, the Devotion to My Heart will be strengthened and, as it were, completed. This Devotion, this Consecration will be, according to My promise, a renovation for My Church, a renewed strength for Christianity which is too often wavering, a source of signal graces for souls, who thereby will be more deeply penetrated with love and confidence."

"The clear light to be granted, through recourse to My Mother, will bring about, above all, the conversion of a multitude of straying and sinful souls: [9] the pity of the Sorrowful and Immaculate Heart of My Mother will implore Mercy for them from My Heart."

---

[9] At Beauraing, nine years earlier, She declared: "I am the Virgin Immaculate" — the Mother of the Heart of gold also said: "I shall convert sinners." The message of the Savior to Berthe Petit, here related, comes to confirm that of Our Lady to the Belgian children.

CHAPTER X

FRANCISCAN TERTIARY: INTERIOR LIFE

IT is not to be wondered at that a dedicated soul — such as Berthe Petit undoubtedly was — should become a member of the Fraternity of the Blessed Sacrament, and subsequently join the Tertiaries of the great St. Francis of Assisi.

Her exile in Switzerland during the War had brought her, as we have seen, to Lucerne. The Convent of the Capuchin Fathers there is the center of a Pilgrimage to Our Lady, the origin of which can be traced back as far as Pentecost Sunday of the year 1531. It was here that Berthe received the little habit on April 2, 1916, from the hands of Father Theodore, in the private chapel of the convent. Here too, she was professed on April 15, 1917.

Her title of Tertiary was very dear to her. She never failed to recite the Little Office, which she came to know by heart, and she always made an effort to practice the Franciscan virtues, especially humility, charity and mortification of the senses. This charity she imbibed from her immense love of the Crucified.

"Everything must be done through charity," she used to say, "because charity goes up to God, who, in turn, pours down on souls all His charity, which is His love."

She did violence to herself to smile, in spite of her terrible sufferings for, "in order to do good," Jesus had confided to her, "it is essential that your soul should blossom forth in smiles of kindliness, and this, notwithstanding all your sufferings, because you are the reflection of the qualities of My Heart." Sympathetic to the trials of others, she was constantly preoccupied with their pain; in her eyes, her own was of no consequence. She gave everything to Jesus and, in a supreme surrender, she added to her vow of victim the vow of "the most perfect."

She always sought to make peace reign in herself and in those around her, but this was not without a struggle. By nature she was quick-tempered and sometimes impatient; she was highly sensitive as is frequently the case with chosen souls. Her ready wit, which was oftentimes piquant, was not slow to detect the amusing side of things out of which she got a good deal of fun.

One could feel she was thoroughly human. Human in the matter of kindness, but human also in this way — that, living only in God, she nevertheless had to overcome her faults just like ordinary people.

Her humility was perfect. She never boasted of the great favors she received. Her greatest desire was to pass unnoticed, and except for her luminous countenance, nothing distinguished her in a crowd, not even in the midst of her own. When asked for advice, she did not give it at once. "I have to recollect myself," she would say, "perhaps I shall be able to answer you tomorrow." It sometimes happened that, at the next interview, she would welcome you with a clear solution which you felt had a supernatural touch. Very often, too, did she say in all humility: "I do not know anything, I have not been enlightened" and for nothing in the world would she say more. She who, every morning, was lost in God, went about afterwards devoting herself to the humble daily duties of the household. She even took care to be neat in her apparel, without any affectation, so that she would not be in any way conspicuous. Always anxious to avoid attention, she had begged God not to give her the stigmata, and her prayer was heard. But her intimate friends knew that on Good Friday and often on other Fridays during the course of the year, the palms of her hands and the soles of her feet caused her cruel suffering. Her lips were torn and bleeding and likewise her tongue. The pains in her head scarcely ever ceased, and her thirst was devouring.

She often said: "We are only instruments; we are God's wisp of straw." How frequently was this counsel heard to fall from her lips: "Let us accept all sufferings: do not ask for them; this would be pride and presumption." It is easy to see the meaning of the words "let us accept" when we recall that towards the end of her life, she admitted that she never had refused anything to Jesus!

Every night, between eleven and twelve, from the age of fifteen, she made the Holy Hour and it was then that Jesus or His Blessed Mother would often manifest themselves to her. It also happened that He would speak during the day, to enlighten her on certain events or about persons who consulted her.

How did Berthe perceive these words?

"They are spoken," she explained, "by a voice so clear and so firm, that they force me to listen and they are impressed on my conscience. I would not hesitate to die in attestation of their truth." In saying this she repeated the thought and the words of Saint Teresa, in the third Chapter of the *Interior Castle:*

> "These words are uttered by a voice so clear that not a syllable is lost, and they are understood more distinctly than if heard by the ears. It rests with ourselves not to listen to human speech, while the word of God is inescapable, sovereignly independent of our own will. It commands a hearing, a perfect attention to all that God wishes to say. The moment the soul hears these words, it no longer hesitates: it would die in attestation of their truth. If, at times, one loses the memory of them, it is owing to the fact that a considerable time has elapsed, or that the words themselves were expressive of tenderness or instruction. For with regard to those involving a prophecy, I do not think that they could be forgotten — at least that has never happened to me, although I have a very poor memory."

Now, Berthe never transmitted any words without having recollected herself in God, so as to be enlightened on points that she might have either overlooked or forgotten — or possibly mistaken. Generally, she remembered exactly what she had heard. It sometimes happened that her Guardian Angel actually whispered to her words which had escaped her and, on certain occasions, Our Lord Himself deigned to repeat whatever He had asked or declared.

One would be surprised at times that certain prophecies were not fulfilled at the time expected, but does not Saint Catherine of Siena, quoting the Sovereign Master, say:

> "Words uttered from Heaven have hardly any relation with those of earth. In the region beyond everything is short and Eternity cannot be compared with this life... What seems to you long to produce is rapid for Me, for I see and order everything and I hold all in My hand."

Obviously, the case is quite different with words proceeding from an over active mind or lively imagination or from a nature not well balanced or overwrought by fasts and vigils that excess of which could be restrained. But this was not so with Berthe who by an act of the divine Will could neither sleep as she wished, or retain any nourishment. Moderation in everything was always her principle.

Berthe had frequent communications with the souls in Purgatory, especially with the souls of priests who had yet to satisfy divine Justice. They often appeared to her at night, to ask for prayers or to announce to her their approaching deliverance. Discretion forbids us to disclose the names of those concerning whom she was thus enlightened.

When the servant of God entered any sanctuary, she was drawn like a magnet to the Altar where the Blessed Sacrament was reserved. Now, in many churches the Sacred Species is reserved in a side chapel, so that it was not the sanctuary lamp that guided her, but the call of the Prisoner of Love.

She could sense the odor of sin in a soul and in this connection she sometimes confessed how repugnant it was to her to be in a crowd.

Her spiritual readings were the Gospel, the *Imitation of Christ,* and one or other treatise on our Blessed Lady. She had read Msgr. Gay, Father Eymard and Madame Swetchine. A favorite of hers was the *Calendar of St. Paul* and she meditated a page each day. "We must live the Mass," she used to say and her Missal never left her. Father Decorsant had turned her away from mystical works. She was interested in history and biography; sometimes (but this was rare) she even read an edifying novel.

During the course of a conversation, everything would interest her — politics, war, music, literature, charitable organizations. She loved her family and often spoke about them.

When, after a period of particularly painful suffering, she was exhausted, the Blessed Virgin would come to her during the night, generally under the form of a lovely blue silhouette, fringed with silver. She would lean over her suffering child and her presence brought "incredible peace."

One day an intimate friend asked her what impression these apparitions made: "It is a great joy to have had them," she answered, "and a great grief to have them no more. Side by side with this great joy, there is a great void, a void much greater than before. But it remains ever a great happiness of soul that Our Lady has deigned to stoop down over a poor human creature."

CHAPTER XI

IMMOLATION OF THE VICTIM

God was making His divine preparations to recall to Himself this predestined soul. When during the summer of 1942, despite the difficulties of travel in time of war, Berthe could go once more to Louvignies in a Red Cross ambulance, she felt, as did all those around her, that it would be her last sojourn there.

At the beginning of her stay the weather was very severe and she was obliged to keep to her room. She was numb with the cold, although a bright fire was burning and it was the middle of August. When anyone pitied her, she would murmur: "It is so good to suffer! How many souls there are to be saved!" And she prayed almost inaudibly: "O Jesus, may I be for ever a crucified victim!"

She had, however, the joy of assisting at the first Mass of a young priest, a native of the village. It was she who, with her pain-racked fingers, prepared the sacred vestments which were presented to him, and which, according to Belgian custom, are carried in procession.

At this time joy returned to a certain family (whom we call D...) in the following circumstances. Here are the mother's own words:

> "Berthe Petit was very fond of our little Antoinette. In July, 1942, after an attack of whooping cough, the child developed pleurisy. Berthe asked her friend Countess de V. to bring her in the invalid carriage to our house. She asked to have our little one, wrapped in a blanket, on her knees. She blessed her saying: "Put her back to bed. I am going to ask the good God to cure her and, if He wills, in four or five days she will be at the table with the family; she will not cough any more and she will be quite well." — Next day, the doctor called again; he could find no more trace of the pleurisy and he noticed that the whooping cough was disappearing. Six days later, our little darling was at the table with us and since then she never had a relapse and she is enjoying perfect health."

Berthe hoped that, during her sojourn at Louvignies, as in preceding years, she would have a vision of Our Lady who always blessed that hospitable abode. This time the Queen of Heaven did not come, but Jesus Himself said to His servant on August 5th: "You have not the consolation of the gentle visit of My Mother, but you have in its fullness that of My abiding love, and therefore your soul should never know disappointment. Do you not feel this consolation which is the strength of your life? Continue to offer up your life of suffering because it leads to the triumph of My Will. The Heart of My Mother will be understood as it ought to be, and the Devotion to her Heart united to Mine will give peace, but true peace so much sought after and yet so little merited."

These words on the subject of peace had already been pronounced on April 25th. And later the Savior added: "You will never know any consolation."

One day, Berthe complained thus to Jesus: —

"Lord, how is it that, while confiding this work to me, you permit it to be thwarted at every moment?"

"You are astonished!" The Divine Master deigned to answer: "Do you forget that My own acts were constantly thwarted and that My Mother always lived in anxiety and suffering? Remain in your way, in spite of darkness and give time for the light to make its appearance."

Back again in Brussels on August 20th, the servant of God, undermined by suffering, continued to decline. The paralysis of the legs became aggravated: it was arthritis of a deforming, swollen type. The pain, bearable at first, became by degrees intolerable....

It was always with that mysterious smile and far-away gaze that she received her intimate friends — members of her family and persons devoted to the Sorrowful and Immaculate Heart of Mary. She spoke very little of herself, but she would listen at length to the account of their trials so that her visitors left with the comfort of peace and light. Hers was the secret that Madame Swetchine also knew: "To have suffered much," she says in her writings of which Berthe was a very keen reader, "is to resemble those who know many languages, to have learned to understand everything, and to make oneself understood by all."

However, the Divine Master after having overwhelmed His

"apostle" with His most precious favors, was pleased to leave her now in darkness and desolation. In this mysterious way He was accomplishing in her a work of supreme purification. His promises concerning the Devotion to the Sorrowful and Immaculate Heart of His Mother were not to human appearances being realized, and His servant was asking herself in self-reproach whether she had been inferior to her task. However, she never doubted the divine word, but her burden of trial would have crushed a soul of less heroic fiber. She felt herself so much alone, deprived as she was of the presence of the Blessed Sacrament in the house — for she was by no means able to walk to the church. And all the time the war was going on its seemingly endless, lamentable course. . . .

The feast of Christmas did not bring her any consolation. Her sacrifice was being accepted in its entirety.

"When you surrendered yourself to Me as a victim," Jesus said to her, "you not only accepted to be united to my whole life and to My Calvary, but also to My sacred Infancy hidden, poor, miserable, deprived of all, and offered as a holocaust."

In spite of excruciating sufferings, even in the limb which remained healthy, Berthe forced herself to welcome her dear ones on January 1, 1943, but it was obvious that she was changing very rapidly and growing weaker. She was being undermined by disease.

No one guessed the cause of these new and intolerable sufferings. She was treated for rheumatism and she had accepted remedies which her stomach could not support, and which in fact made her grievously ill. At length it was her surgeon, called in as a last resort, who found the cause of her pain. An X-ray revealed spontaneous double fracture of the left leg, the leg which up to this time had been healthy.

For weeks, therefore, she had been trying to hobble along on a broken limb. It had to be put in plaster and she was ordered to remain practically motionless. Still she never lay in bed. Pulmonary stagnation was feared and its symptoms appeared towards the end of February. From this time forward, a nurse came, each morning, to help with her toilet. She never demanded further assistance, and she insisted that she did not wish to trouble anyone during the night.

Towards the middle of March, the surgeon removed the plaster and left only a gaiter around the leg but the patient became so weak that this weight was troublesome. She was often drowsy during the day and could not hold long conversations, but the very mention of the graces obtained through the Devotion to the Sorrowful and Immaculate Heart would bring a smile to her lips. One could feel that she was, little by little, withdrawing and freeing herself from material things. She never spoke of her approaching end. That day seemed of no importance completely lost as she was in the Will of God.

From the time of her arrival at the Rue Joseph Stallaert, Holy Communion was brought to her every day, with great devotedness, by an auxiliary priest of the Missions; Father Kn . . . When he was not able to attend, a curate came from the parish or a professor from the neighboring college. Canon A . . . replaced Canon Cr . . . who had become her director after the death of Bishop Legraive.

It was her parish priest, Father C . . . , who brought her the Holy Oils (this was her eleventh time to be anointed) invoking on the patient all the blessings of Our Lady of the Sorrowful and Immaculate Heart. That ceremony was unforgettable.

Now, for the first time, Berthe remained in bed and henceforth she was never to leave it. Her heart was giving way and she had painful attacks of suffocation whenever, devoured by thirst, she absorbed a few drops of liquid. Her mouth and tongue became coated with thrush. A film came over her eyes, the whole of her poor body was one mass of suffering and her head, not finding any rest on the pillow, fell sorrowfully forward like that of Christ on the Cross. Like Him, too, her swollen deformed lips murmured: "I thirst. I thirst." Swelling set in, and her countenance was by now beyond recognition.

The last two nights as Countess de V. and her faithful maid Anna were alternately watching by her bed, this plaintive cry "I thirst" never ceased. The patient was devoured by a consuming interior fire which nothing could appease. This thirst she had endured all her life, and Cardinal Mercier knew it well, for he had granted Berthe an indulgence of 50 days every time she pronounced the word "Sitio," knowing that it expressed her thirst for the souls of sinners as well as for those of priests for whom she had offered herself entirely.

Until her death, Holy Communion remained the only interval of solace in suffering: towards the end she could absorb only a very small particle. One could feel that she was over-whelmed with pain and that she had already entered into a mysterious agony. On receiving the Holy Eucharist, her countenance reflected the complete serenity of her soul, now so far away that even to speak to her of God would be to disturb her divine colloquy.

However, on Thursday, March 25th, Feast of the Annunciation, she was informed that the Act of Consecration to the Immaculate Heart of Mary had been read in the Cathedral of Sainte Gudule in Brussels, in the midst of a great concourse. She smiled at the thought of the glory being given to Our Lady, and when with prophetic gaze into the future she remarked: "It will be done." She was thinking of that other Consecration to the *Sorrowful* and Immaculate Heart, which had been the aim of her whole life.

Contrary to the general expectation, the "apostle" of the Blessed Virgin did not die on the glorious day of the Annunciation. That day was again spent in suffering and in great cardiac agitation. In the afternoon, she said simply: "It will not be for today." That night was extremely painful.

She was often heard calling for her mother. Now, March 26th was the anniversary of the death of Madame Petit and the Divine Master was to call her daughter on that same day. Suddenly Berthe cried out with a very strong voice, not at all like that of a dying person: "I desire it to be known that I am entirely submissive to all that the good God wills."

From 3 p.m. to 4 p.m. the end seemed at hand and the cry "I thirst. Give me to drink!" was heartrending. Then the patient became calm and began to dose. By six o'clock she was sleeping peacefully — her head having at last found a support on the pillow. Her breathing was regular, and her pulse strong and steady. Everything looked as though the fatal issue would be delayed. At six o'clock the Countess de V., who was watching, left the room for a short time. Returning after five minutes, she noticed with surprise that the rhythm of the breathing had subsided. She bent down closer only to ascertain that the "apostle" of the Virgin of the Dolors had left this earth. God had come to take this soul and had given it to His Mother. He had taken her on a Friday, in all the austerity of her suffering. No doubt as her body bent under its weight, her soul for three hours remained on Calvary, beside Our Lady of

Dolors and St. John, to awake at length in Light Eternal amid the never ending Hosanna! . . .

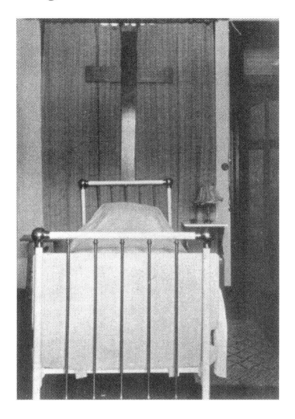

Berthe Petit's bed in which she breathed her last.

Many years previous, Berthe had said to her friend Countess de V., at the castle of Louvignies: "When I die, you will be near me and you will prepare me for burial." This was fulfilled to the letter.

Majestic on her funeral couch, Berthe laid there for three days, surrounded by lilies, a drapery of white lace framing her delicate face. Her features had taken on an incomparable beauty. At the head of the bed stood a great bare cross, just as Jesus had formerly shown it to her in a vision; it was surmounted by the crown of thorns, typical of the one which, forty-four years previously, Saint Catherine of Siena had placed upon her head. "I love the cross like that," she had said one day, "I wanted it so and I had it made purposely without the figure of Christ, for it *is I myself who am to be nailed to it in His place.*"

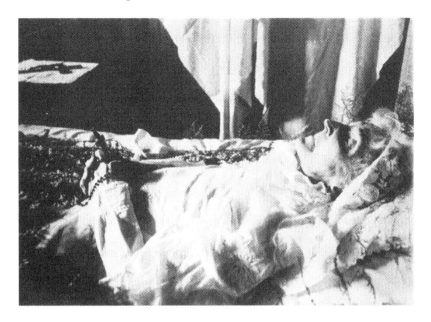

Berthe Petit on her deathbed

The news of her death spread like lightning, and with it the story of the extraordinary graces of which she had been the recipient and of which very few people were till then aware. Even her own family did not know of these favors. For five days her apartment was invaded by a concourse of pious people: the greater number were strangers; they sprang up from everywhere, deeply affected at the thought that a "saint" had died here. They arrived laden with flowers, and they touched the corpse with rosaries, medals and pictures of the Sorrowful Heart. Several of the clergy also came to kneel at the foot of the bed of her, who in the flower of youth, had offered herself as victim for the sanctification of priests.

The obsequies took place on the 31st in the Church of the Annunciation; then the cortege left for the little village of Louvignies (Hainaut) where the deceased had expressed the wish to rest beneath the shadow of the bell-tower. The good people of the village, whom she had so often consoled, and the children whom she had so dearly loved were there to receive her.

These humble folk had likewise brought pious objects with which they touched her coffin and they said amongst themselves: "No harm will befall us now Mlle. Petit is resting in our midst." Indeed, the village was miraculously protected at the time of the German retreat.

Inside the chapel (Louvignies). On the right is the big cross which was at the head of Berthe Petit's bed.

Vox populi, vox Dei!

On April 8th following, a Requiem Mass was celebrated at the request of the clients of the Devotion in the Church of the Annunciation in Brussels. They were a numerous and most devout congregation. On leaving the church, all of them spoke of the favors obtained from the *Sorrowful and Immaculate Heart,* through the intercession of Mary's faithful servant.

Since then, these favors are beyond reckoning. [10]

By a mysterious design of Divine Providence, she whom Jesus had chosen to make known this Devotion so dear to His Heart, was to see here below its preparatory steps but not its triumph. It is thus with all precursors. "In the hour of triumph" the Savior had said, "it will be seen that *I alone have inspired,* in my chosen instruments, a Devotion similar to that with which My Heart is honored. IT IS AS A SON THAT I HAVE CONCEIVED THIS DEVOTION IN HONOR OF MY MOTHER. IT IS AS GOD THAT I IMPOSE IT."

The Reverend Father Kn . . . of the Society of the African Missions, was good enough to give, on June 2, 1943, this attestation which outlines, in a striking way, the Eucharistic life of the servant of God: —

"For six years I brought Holy Communion to Mlle. Petit and I witnessed day to day, to my great edification, what a holy soul she was and how the Eucharist was for her the viaticum of each day. To bring her Holy Communion was my joy. Most probably you think it must be so for any priest, whose principal function is the administration of the Sacraments. But remember, however, that I have been a missionary for many years on the Gold Coast, which is the most trying country on the face of the earth. Its climate can be ruinous to health, and it has not spared mine, so much so that I suffer every day, especially in the morning, from malaria and asthma. It will thus be easily understood how difficult it was to fulfill this priestly ministry towards Mlle. Petit!"

"It was not so much the idea of fulfilling my priestly ministry that gave me this joy, as the fact that I was to bring my Jesus to a soul supernaturalized — one who was living only through Him and suffering for Him alone."

"Having sometimes to replace a member of the parish clergy for one of the regular Masses, it would happen that the patient did not get Holy Communion at the usual hour. I myself felt pain on this account: — I knew that, for many hours, she had been waiting for the Bread of Life with a real "eucharistic hunger." As I drew near the room where she

---

[10] Those who receive favors are requested to send a detailed account to the Mother Superior of the Camaldolese nuns, La Seyne-sur-Mer (Var) France, or to the Secretariat de la Devotion, 17, rue Guimard, Bruxelles, Belgium. The center of the Devotion in France is now at the Sanctuary of La Seyne-sur-Mer.

awaited the Host, I could hear her sighing for Holy Communion. As soon as she had received the Sacred Species, the hunger of her soul would be appeased. After each Communion her spirit seemed to leave this world. It was, in fact, the 'great event' of the day. For this she had prepared during the long hours of insomnia and to the very end she lived on the Bread of Life. I shall never forget her last Communion."

"On March 25th, it seemed to me that Mlle. Petit was slightly better. She had found it less difficult than the day before to receive the divine Particle — about the tenth of a

The chapel in Louvignies under which Berthe Petit lies buried. It is the vault of the family of the Countess de Villegas de Ste. Pierre.

normal Host. She was to die, however, on Friday, March 26th. That morning, I had the impression that this would be her last Communion. When I was there with the Sacred Species, close to her lips, she was not immediately aware of my presence. Suddenly she revived and, as usual, joined her hands to receive Holy Communion. She had great difficulty in parting her lips. . . . After Communion, she cried aloud and in a strong voice "I thirst!" Several times she repeated these words of the dying Christ."

"At that moment I understood something of the anguish with which Jesus must have pronounced this word on the Cross. . . . It was the last time that Mlle. Petit received the Blessed Sacrament."

CHAPTER XII

DEVOTION TO THE SORROWFUL AND IMMACULATE HEART OF MARY

I.—THEOLOGICAL JUSTIFICATION

No one could doubt either the sound theological basis or the excellence of the Devotion to the "Sorrowful and Immaculate Heart of Mary."

We must admit that her "Sorrowful Heart" is the center so to speak, of all the suffering which the Mother of God endured for our salvation. We speak of the Heart of "Our Lady of the Seven Dolors," symbolically pierced by a sword, according to the prophecy of the venerable Simeon; it was driven by that same thrust of the lance that pierced the Heart of her Son nailed to the Cross, at the foot of which she was standing. "Juxta crucem Jesu Mater ejus" says the sacred text.

The profound significance of this scene, the most touching of the Passion, has never been lost sight of by the Church and by the faithful. The Precious Blood of Christ, human Blood, but Blood unique and divine in its absolute purity, flowed to the very last drop from the summit of the Cross for the redemption of the world. It had its immaculate source in the *Heart of Mary, His Mother.*

This same Blood, burning with love in the divine Heart of the Son of Man broken by our sins, burned with the same fire and the same love in the sorrowful and pure Heart of His Mother. If our hearts were not so often hardened by sin, we ourselves would burn with love for this divine Mother, for Jesus, at the moment He was expiring, bequeathed Her to us as our Mother, that she might beget us in sorrow, and through her sorrows, lead us to Life Eternal.

For this reason the Church has held steadfastly to the commemoration of the co-redemptive sufferings of the Blessed Virgin, by instituting the Feast of Our Lady of the Seven Dolors, also known as the Feast of the Compassion, the Office of which is one of the most beautiful and touching of the Liturgy. The Sorrows of Mary could not be recalled with more evangelical simplicity and more eloquence than we find in the "*Stabat Mater Dolorosa,*" the sequence of the Mass of the Compassion, and in the vesper hymn of the same day: "*O quot undis lacrymarum.*" The haunting sorrow of these two liturgical poems cannot fail to touch deeply those who ponder on them in loving contemplation.

Finally, the Church has once again stressed the capital importance of the Immaculate Mother in our Redemption by describing her in the Litany as "Queen of Martyrs." Anyone who suffers in conformity with Christ collaborates in the redemption of the world by Christ. This is affirmed by a Decree — that of the *Communion of Saints.* Now, which of the saints has shared in the sufferings and death of Christ with more intensity, with more perfect conformity than the Blessed Virgin in Him, through Him, for Him and with Him?

There is no need to insist further: the Devotion to the Sorrowful and Immaculate Heart of Mary is perfectly traditional, and therefore orthodox.

With regard to the title "Sorrowful and Immaculate Heart of Mary," is it astonishing that the Savior wishes the word "Sorrowful" to precede that of "Immaculate" in the invocation to the Heart of the Virgin-Mother?

Our Lord to whom all glory is due by virtue of the hypostatic union — and no other cause of glory could be more noble — said to the disciples on the way to Emmaus, after the Resurrection: "Ought not Christ to have suffered these things, and so enter into His glory?" It is therefore by title of His sufferings rather than by that of the infinitely more noble hypostatic union that Christ claims to enter into His glory.

The Blessed Virgin, in like manner, to whom all glory and love are due by reason of her title of Mother of God, would have the children of this earth fix their gaze more upon her sorrows than upon her privileges.

This preference is proved by yet another consideration. Jesus Christ, revealing His Heart to Saint Margaret Mary, brings into relief not so much the love He has for His Heavenly Father, but His love for mankind — a love *suffering,* ignored and despised. It is His Heart pierced and crowned with thorns that He offers to our direct worship, thus drawing our attention to His sufferings.

It is but natural to assume that Providence should ordain the mission of Mary on lines corresponding to that of her divine Son. It is equally to her Sorrowful Heart that Our Lord wishes to call our attention. Side by side with the pierced Heart of the Savior, there must be the Sorrowful Heart of the Co-Redemptrix, the one and the other transpierced because of their love for ungrateful mankind.

If the revelations of Berthe Petit are deserving of credence, it is the Will of the Savior that the word "Sorrowful" precede that of "Immaculate" in the invocation He recommended. This stresses the perfect association of the Heart of Mary with that of Jesus. When we say "Immaculate" we glorify God in Mary. When we say "Sorrowful" we glorify Mary in God.

Here is the whole secret of the Devotion. In conclusion, therefore, without the slightest doubt, from the point of view of dogma and according to all demands of Marian Theology, there is *nothing contrary* to the spreading, encouraging and amplifying of the Devotion. The great tide of faith, hope and charity already flowing in the *Mystical Body of Christ* is beginning to surge everywhere — only too eager to rise aloft with ardor to the *Sorrowful and Immaculate Heart of Mary.* This ascending movement has all the more impetus to expansion by the fact that, during and since the first World War, very learned and eminent ecclesiastics (amongst them a Pope as we have seen earlier) have invited the faithful to make use of the invocation "Sorrowful and Immaculate Heart of Mary, pray for us who have recourse to Thee."

II.—GROWTH OF THE DEVOTION

In the course of the year 1942, Berthe Petit felt her strength steadily declining. Our Lord gave her to understand that she would not have the consolation of seeing the official triumph of the Devotion of which she was the "apostle," but that the hour had come to bring this Devotion to the notice of the faithful by means of pamphlets and the wide distribution of copies of the picture of His Holy Mother venerated at the Convent of Ollignies.

This picture, somewhat mysterious in its origin, was discovered at the time of the armistice of 1918 in the cellars of the boarding school conducted by the Bernardine Nuns where Berthe had been educated. On the departure of the troops one of the nuns was putting the place again in order. She found apiece of cardboard on which was pasted a pornographic

The Virgin of Ollignies

picture which she tore off to consign it to the flames. To her great astonishment she saw that it was covering a very beautiful representation of the Blessed Virgin! The Community put this in a place of honor and soon experienced that prayer before it brought signal favors.

Various indications prove that it is of French origin. When Berthe returned from Switzerland, where she had been during the War, and saw the picture in 1919, she recognized at once the two-fold symbol of the Virgin of the *Sorrowful and Immaculate Heart.*

The picture represents the Mother of God holding in her left hand a lily, symbol of her immaculate purity, the gratuitous gift of her Son, while the index of the right hand, resting on her breast, draws and fixes attention to her Sorrowful Heart, surrounded by flames and transpierced with a sword. The deep and far-seeing gaze of the Immaculate seems to contemplate with sadness the sins of the world — cause of the sufferings expressed on her gentle face which is leaning towards the right. The features resemble those of the *Pieta* (Sorrowful Virgin) so well known in most churches.

On April 25, 1942, Our Lord, making allusion to the increasing tempo of the war, said: "A frightful torment is in preparation. It will be seen that the forces launched with such fury, will soon be let loose. It is, now or never, the moment for all of you to give yourselves to the Sorrowful and Immaculate Heart of My Mother. By her acceptance of Calvary My Mother has participated in all My sufferings. Devotion to her Heart united to Mine will bring peace, that true peace, so often implored and yet so little merited."

In obedience to the commands of the Divine Master, Berthe and her friends lost no time in propagating the picture already referred to. It bore on the obverse side the invocation so dear to Cardinal Mercier and indulgenced by him and on the reverse side the form of Consecration used by Cardinal Bourne and which has, in addition, the imprimatur of the Bishopric of Tournai.

These pictures were, in a short time, widely spread and in demand everywhere in Belgium. When at the end of 1942, Marian solemnities were being widely celebrated to obtain peace and parishes and religious communities were, in accordance with the wishes of the Sovereign Pontiff, being consecrated to the *Immaculate Heart,* it was found that many of them had, in fact, been already consecrated to the *Sorrowful and Immaculate Heart.* The invocation so dear to Cardinal Mercier and to Cardinal Bourne was already well known.

III.—PROGRESS

The picture of the Virgin of Ollignies is now spread the world over: printings of it adorn many churches; newly founded bells are dedicated to the Sorrowful and Immaculate Heart; chapels are consecrated to it and the first church, under this title, has just been built in France, at La Seyne-sur-Mer (Var).

Missionaries writing from the burning regions of the Congo, from the Philippine Islands, Japan, Burma, Vietnam, Haiti, Morocco, Algeria, Brazil as well as from regions of the Great North bear witness that their flocks are affected by the Sorrows of the Mother of God and they point out how much these Sorrows draw souls to a deeper understanding of the beauty and the mystery of her co-redemption.

Ardent apostles are arising in the United States, in Canada, in Spain and Portugal, in Egypt, in England, in Switzerland, in Italy, in Holland and in Corsica. In *Belgium,* one of the first solemn manifestations in honor of the Devotion goes back as far as December 10, 1944, when Mr. van den Corput, Governor of Luxembourg, read the form of consecration of his Province, in the name of his colleagues, in the Church of St. Martin at Arlon, His Excellency, Bishop Charrue, Bishop of Namur, presided at this ceremony. He begged the merciful protection of the Sorrowful and Immaculate Heart of Mary for the king, the royal family and the whole of Belgium. A few days later, General von Rundstedt launched his offensive. The town of Arlon was spared, although the Province of Luxembourg suffered terrible ravages. But Belgium was saved, thanks to the counterattack launched by General Patton, who implored the help of God before starting the campaign.

Cardinal van Roey, Primate of Belgium, who always showed benevolence to Berthe Petit and recommended himself to her prayers, found the Devotion "irreproachable and excellent." As an indication of his encouragement, His Eminence doubled the indulgence granted to the invocation by his predecessor Cardinal Mercier.

On July 18, 1948, Bishop Boone, Dean of the Collegiate Church of St. Gudule, solemnly consecrated the city of Brussels from the Cathedral steps, in the presence of the Apostolic Nuncio, now Cardinal Cento.

The Reverend Father Perbal, S.J., has organized a very fruitful campaign for the *Fireside Marian Missions.* A small statue of Our Lady of Fatima showing her Heart pierced with thorns is carried from house to house to give its message of prayer and penance. Before its departure, the head of the house is requested to read aloud the Act of Consecration on behalf of the family.

In all these pilgrimages, especially at Lourdes, at Pontmain, at Banneux, on the occasion of "Journées des Malades" and in Hospitals, the prayer of the *Consecration of the Sick* composed by Dom Eugene Vandeur, O.S.B., is recited with intense fervor. Several bishops have granted an indulgence of 100 days to this prayer.

It is to Dom Willibrord de Wilde, O.S.B., that we owe the *Marian Crusade through the Mass;* thus he hopes to obtain from God, through the all-powerful and universal mediation of the Sorrowful and Immaculate Heart of Mary, the conversion and the peace of the world.

The Crusade of the *Decade of the Rosary,* which is followed by the invocation, recited at night prayer for the conversion of sinners, is gaining followers by the thousand in every country. The center is at the Convent of the Missionary Canonesses of St. Augustin, at Heverlé, near Louvain. This center also propagates the *Consecration of Families* to which Bishop Kerkhofs, Bishop of Liége, and Bishop Himmer, Bishop of Tournai, have each granted 100 days indulgence.

The World League of Reparation to the Sorrowful and Immaculate Heart of Mary is directed in Belgium by the Abbé Chantraine-Soheit-Tinlot (Prov. of Liége). [11] The members undertake to recite the Rosary every day; to make a daily sacrifice however small; to celebrate the first Saturday of the month by a Communion of Reparation offered in honor of the Sorrowful and Immaculate Heart of Mary, and to meditate on this day, for a quarter of an hour, on any of the mysteries of

---

[11] Actually by Abbé Halleux, at Charneux.

the Rosary. All this intercession is offered up for the conversion of Russia and for world peace.

During the Marian Year the Devotion was given a considerable impetus by the consecration of numerous parishes. On Pentecost Sunday His Excellency, Bishop Himmer, solemnly consecrated his clergy to the Sorrowful and Immaculate Heart in the course of a beautiful ceremony in the Cathedral. He invited all religious communities to recite, on the day of their renovation of vows, the Act of Consecration composed by Mére Montfalin, Portuguese Religious of the Congregation of St. Dorothy. On December 8th, the Bishop consecrated his whole diocese. Simultaneously, in every parish, the clergy, united with their flocks, proclaimed their joy in consecrating themselves "to your Sorrowful Heart, O Mary, who acquired this title by participating in the Passion of Jesus and thus collaborating in our redemption: to your Immaculate Heart, full of the grace of God, overflowing with His charity, radiating with purity and with every perfection."

Moreover, His Excellency invited the priests of the diocese, and this from the very beginning of the Marian Year, to recite the following invocation after Mass: "Sorrowful and Immaculate Heart of Mary, intercede for us."

His Excellency, Bishop Kerkhofs, Bishop of Liége, similarly consecrated his clergy during a beautiful ceremony on October 5, 1954, in the Basilica of Our Lady of Tongres.

FRANCE

France was specially conspicuous in spreading the Devotion, of which the center for propaganda was originally at Issoudun. It is now transferred to La Seyne-sur-Mer (Var) where the first church dedicated to the Sorrowful and Immaculate Heart of Mary has been erected.

Bishop Richaux, Bishop of Laval, consecrated his diocese on July 17, 1947, and on August 15, 1948, the town of Laval itself during a commemorative ceremony in the Basilica of Avesniéres. His successor, Bishop Rousseau, renewed this gesture very solemnly on August 15, 1951. Moreover, Bishop Richaux, who became Archbishop of Bordeaux, attached an indulgence of 200 days to the following prayer: "Oh! Lord, my God, I beg the protection of your merciful love for suffering humanity so that, repentant, it may turn to you wholeheartedly through the infinite merits of the Most Precious Blood of your Divine Son and the mediation of the Sorrowful and Immaculate Heart of Mary."

A great *National Day of the Sick,* presided over by Bishop Rousseau, takes place every year in July at Pontmain. All the invalids there are consecrated to the Sorrowful and Immaculate Heart. From the whole of France, Belgium, Luxembourg, Italy, Spain, Switzerland, thousands of others join from afar in this consecration to the recital of which an indulgence of 100 days was granted by the Bishop of Laval.

The *Consecration of a Child* and the *Consecration of a Family* are both very popular. The text of the latter comes from the Visitation Convent of Paray-le-Monial; it is also well known in Belgium and has been indulgenced by Bishop Himmer.

Each year since 1950, France has been consecrated on August 15th to the Sorrowful and Immaculate Heart in the Church of Our Lady of Victories in Paris. At the yearly processional commemoration of the Vow of Louis XIII, February 10, 1638, the Consecration is renewed.

The Camaldolese Religious, who are in charge of the Devotion since 1959, have been publishing a quarterly Bulletin *L'APPEL du Coeur Douloureux et Immaculé de MARIE* which is very much appreciated. It gives liturgical articles and all news concerning the Devotion.

ENGLAND

England loves to recall over the radio each year the extraordinary victory gained on September 15, 1940 (Feast of Our Lady of Dolors). On that day a small group of young pilots destroyed 185 enemy aircraft intended to be the spearhead of the invasion. From that time forward the day-light attacks of the Luftwaffe ceased.

The indulgence of 100 days which had been granted to the invocation was extended by Cardinal Griffin, on June 21, 1947, to 300 days.

PORTUGAL

The affinity between the apparitions on June 13, 1917, of

Lucy, the seer of Fatima, and the revelations to Berthe Petit is so keenly appreciated in Portugal, that a translation of the biography of the servant of God has been made and published by the Reverend Dom Manuel Cordoso, secretary of the Bishop of Coimbra.

The Diocese of Lamego has been consecrated to the Sorrowful and Immaculate Heart, as also the convents of the Portuguese Nuns of St. Dorothy whose Mother Provincial Montfalin (Dona Eugenia de Souza e Holstein) had known Berthe Petit in Switzerland during the First World War, when her Community was exiled from Portugal. It was at that time that Mother Montfalin composed an Act of Consecration for Religious Communities. Many years later, Bishop Himmer recommended it to the convents of his diocese, to be said when the nuns made their Act of Renewal of Vows on November 21, 1954.

The Blue Army of Fatima, whose Center for Belgium is at 83, rue Archimede, at Bruxelles, has adopted the invocation and the picture of the Virgin of Fatima, the Heart pierced by thorns, thus "Sorrowful."

We realize, more and more, how much the Devotion to the Sorrowful Heart and that of Fatima are all one. The Bishop of Leiria has given proof of this in writing in 1961 to his brothers in the Episcopate telling them to ask the pilgrims who will go there on the 12th and the 13th of October, to make a special effort of prayer and penance in reparation for so many sins, which are the cause of affliction to the Sacred Heart of Jesus and that of the Sorrowful and Immaculate Heart of His Mother. The invocation to the Sorrowful and Immaculate Heart of Mary is popular at Fatima.

SPAIN

In Madrid, the Crusade of the Decade of the Rosary for sinners, followed by the invocation to the Sorrowful and Immaculate Heart of Mary is spreading in a wonderful way.

ITALY

The Trappist Fathers of Tre Fontane in Rome, have had medals struck, and are issuing numerous leaflets to make the

Devotion known. They have also made artistic reproductions in color of the Virgin of Ollignies. Here also is published the *Messageo del S. Cuore di Gesu in favore del Cuore Addolorato di Maria.*

A brochure on Berthe Petit, Messenger of the Sorrowful and Immaculate Heart of Mary has been published in Italian by the Propaganda Mariana — Casa Missione, Casalmonferrato (Alessandria) 1952.

ALGERIA

Thousands of families are being consecrated to the Sorrowful and Immaculate Heart of Mary.

MOROCCO

On December 7, 1954, His Grace, Archbishop Lefébure, Archbishop of Rabat, consecrated his Archdiocese to the Sorrowful and Immaculate Heart of Mary.

CANADA

If there is one country more than another where Our Lady is honored, it is certainly Canada. The beautiful review *Marie* published in Quebec by Roger O'Brien is in itself sufficient evidence of this. In the July 1952 number, there was a remarkable article, profusely illustrated, on the Devotion. Its author is Rev. Fr. Hermann Morin, editor of the *Annales de N.D. du Cap.* This review has frequent news items concerning the Sorrowful and Immaculate Heart.

On April 30, 1953, His Eminence, Cardinal Leger, consecrated the Diocese of Montreal to the Sorrowful and Immaculate Heart. The consecration of the Diocese of Edmundston, by His Excellency, Bishop Tanon, took place on August 15th following.

The invocation "Sorrowful and Immaculate Heart of Mary, pray for us" adorns the porch of the Church of Our Lady in Montreal. It is in large letters and is beautifully illuminated at night by neon lights.

The Director of "Montmarte Canadien" at Quebec, the Reverend Dr. Godbout, has published a special edition of 10,000 copies of the *Life and Revelations of Berthe Petit*. An article by Fr. Morin entitled *The Sorrowful and Immaculate Heart revealed at Fatima* has been printed in leaflet form, and thousands of copies have been distributed. A leaflet *Sacrilege and Blasphemy which pierce the Hearts of Jesus and Mary* has likewise been published.

All the various formulae of Consecration to the Sorrowful and Immaculate Heart of Mary are much in honor in Canada.

A Mission dedicated to Our Lady under the same title was founded in 1953 in the snowy regions of the North Pole. Its founder is the Rev. Fr. Henry, O.M.I.

UNITED STATES

The reviews *Fatima Findings* and *Soul* frequently carry news concerning the Devotion. At the time of the Solemn Sessions of the Blue Army at Plainfield, New Jersey, in 1953, held under the direction of the parish priest the Very Reverend Monsignor Colgan, the Rev. Fr. Ryan, director of *Fatima Findings,* gave a lecture on the Devotion and suggested that all the members of the Blue Army the world over should frequently recite in the course of the day the invocation "Blessed be the Sorrowful and Immaculate Heart of the Virgin Mary." This suggestion was received with such enthusiasm that, thenceforward, every session of the Congress commenced and ended with this prayer. The *Blue Army* has published a short biography of Berthe Petit in English.

The Conventual Franciscan Friars of Marytown, Kenosha, Wisconsin, are publishing, besides this complete biography, the *Act of Consecration to the Sorrowful and Immaculate Heart of Mary* used by Cardinal Bourne, in leaflet form. The Friars are also publishing an illustrated *Novena of Confidence and Thanksgiving to the Sorrowful and Immaculate Heart of Mary.* The Novena is translated from the French edition published by the French Center of the Devotion at La Seyne-sur-Mer.

ECUADOR

The two capital towns of the Republic of Ecuador — Quito and Guayaquil — were consecrated with great splendor in 1952 to the Heart of Mary. This ceremony took place before a picture of Our Lady of Fatima of the thorn-pierced Heart, thus affirming that the Mother of Sorrows is their refuge, and that, through her, the country has returned to her Son. All this took place following the miracle of the picture of Our Lady of the Seven Dolors when, in 1906, at the Jesuit College, Quito, the image opened and closed its eyes, obviously in an effort to restrain its tears.

REUNION ISLANDS

At Salazié, a Parish is consecrated to the Sorrowful and Immaculate Heart since 1952.

SAIGON

To the Redemptorist Fathers of Saigon has been assigned the translation of the Act of Consecration into Vietnamese. The Devotion is gaining ground.

CONGO

A Chapel in honor of the Sorrowful and Immaculate Heart of Mary has been erected at Simba — Prefecture of Bikoro. Lake Tumba.

At Banneux-Notre Dame, Bishop Bihirumwami consecrated his diocese of Ruanda on November 21, 1953. — In the prayer for Families at Nyundo, the Sorrowful and Immaculate Heart of Mary was implored to "spread abundantly amongst our brothers and sisters of Ruanda, the gifts of faith, hope and charity, the light which will never fail and the Love of God, the only good which will never cease."

On October 16, 1960, Bishop Kimbondo of Kisantu, during a beautiful ceremony, in the presence of his excellency, Archbishop Mijaiski-Perelli, Apostolic Delegate to the Congo, and Archbishop Scalais of Leopoldville, and Auxiliary Bishop Malula, consecrated his diocese to the Sorrowful and Immaculate Heart of Mary.

On October 29, 1961, the solemn Consecration of the Diocese of Goma (Kivu) by His Excellency, Bishop Busimba, took place. The original picture of Ollignies, the property of the Bernardine Dames who have a mission in Goma, was carried in procession.

Bishop Verbille of Beruizza, Vicar Apostolic of Fort-Rousset, is spreading the Devotion in his Vicariate.

INDIA

In the East Indies, Fr. Shouriah, S.J., of the Sirkali Mission (Tanjore District), who was miraculously cured by Our Lady of the Sorrowful and Immaculate Heart, [12] became a very ardent apostle. He translated the biography of Berthe Petit into four different Hindu dialects as well as into the English language. The Crusade of the Decade of the Rosary for poor sinners, accompanied by the invocation, has now thousands of members.

The Archbishop of Calcutta has introduced the Devotion into his archdiocese; the Bishop of Mellore has done likewise.

BURMA

Bishop Faliere, Vicar Apostolic of Mandalay, consecrated his diocese on August 15, 1954.

HAITI

At Port of Peace, intense propaganda, thanks to His Excellency, Bishop Guio, and also to a de Montfort Father, Father Chabot, Curate of the Cathedral, the diocese has already been consecrated twice.

At Burundi in Usumburi, thanks to Father B., S.J. (a native) the Devotion has intensified and a temporary chapel has been built awaiting the erection of a large Sanctuary.

---

[12] See Appendix.

CHAPTER XIII

THE APPEALS OF OUR LADY
(from 1830 to the present day)

We have the well substantiated evidence of events — declared by the competent ecclesiastical authority as worthy of credence — by which we can discern various manifestations of the Sorrowful and Immaculate Heart of Mary. Not however *in words,* such as those at Fatima — where the direct object was the Sorrowful and Immaculate Heart; but rather *in fact* — by gestures and attitudes manifesting a Heart Sorrowful and Immaculate. The indication is clear in the case of the Miraculous Medal, La Salette, Lourdes, Pontmain, Beauraing, Banneux and, more recently, Syracuse.

It is of abiding interest to the faithful to have a thorough knowledge of these apparitions and so be able to discern in them what is essentially important. Here we shall limit ourselves to indicating the facts that are directly related to the *Sorrowful* Heart of the Mother of the Savior.

I
THE MIRACULOUS MEDAL

The Miraculous Medal was revealed to Catherine Labouré, novice of the Sisters of Charity, rue du Bac, Paris, on November 27, 1830.

During the course of the second phase of the apparition, there formed around Our Lady an oval shaped picture on which stood out in letters of gold: "O Mary, conceived without sin, pray for us who have recourse to Thee." Soon after, the hands of Our Lady, laden with graces which were symbolized by rays, were lowered and slightly extended. Then the picture was seen to turn around. On the reverse side, Catherine Labouré beheld the first letter of the word "MARY" — a capital M the downstrokes of which were interlaced with the base of a cross. A little lower, two Hearts were shown, the one on the left surrounded by a crown of thorns, *the other on the right, transpierced by a sword* — the Hearts of Jesus and Mary. All around the picture there was a constellation of stars.

Our Lady then said: "Have a medal struck on this model.

Those who wear it will receive great graces."

By showing her Heart transpierced by a sword, Mary prepared the way for the Devotion to the SORROWFUL and Immaculate Heart.

II
OUR LADY OF LA SALETTE

On September 19, 1864 (in that year the eve of the Feast of Our Lady of the Seven Dolors) two illiterate shepherd children, Maximin and Málanie, suddenly saw a beautiful Lady coming forth from a luminous globe. She was seated, her head between her hands, and "her tears were flowing to the ground."

She was weeping over the sins of the world. "If my people do not submit, I will be forced to let go the arm of my Son. It is so heavy that I can no longer hold it back . . . I have given you six days during which you may work, He said. I have reserved the seventh for myself, and you will not devote it to me! . . . The men who drive their carts cannot swear without calling in vain the Holy Name of my Son. These are the two things which weigh His arm down. If the harvest is bad, it is no one's fault but your own. I pointed out this to you last year in what happened to the potato crop; you have not heeded it; on the contrary, when you came across bad ones, you swore by my Son's Name. They will continue to rot and by Christmas this year there will be no more."

Mary was weeping because she saw the punishment reserved for her ungrateful people — like a mother would who has tried everything to convince her guilty children and who has only one more argument left — to burst into tears before them.

No doubt, Mary in glory can no longer be sad any more than the Sacred Heart, or actually cry. But the sins of men are an abomination to God and His Holy Mother. Long ago, when on earth, they wept at the thought of them and now when they have a message to impart, they have no more realistic way of showing their horror of sin than to appear sad or to shed tears. The tears of Our Lady are caused by men's contempt of the rights of God as they are summed up in the first words of the Our Father "Hallowed be Thy Name; Thy Kingdom come." Instead of this, men blaspheme at every turn and do not keep holy the Lord's Day. A christian people which will not submit: an angry God Who will strike: an incomparable Mother who unfolds all the compassion of her loving and SORROWFUL Heart to reconcile her earthly children with her Child in Heaven — such is the essential meaning of the message of La Salette. It is obvious that it has lost nothing of its objective reality.

(P. Pl. Chevalier, M.S.C.)

III
OUR LADY OF LOURDES

Not alone the Alps, but the Pyrenees also have served the Queen of Heaven as pedestal, thus showing her predilection for France.

In all, there were to be 18 apparitions to little Bernadette Soubirous.

The first was on February 11, 1858. Bernadette, collecting faggots for fuel near the Grotto of Massabielle, suddenly beheld a young and beautiful Lady in a golden cloud "more beautiful than ever I saw," as she related afterwards.

On February 21st, the Lady said: "Pray for sinners."

On the 24th: *"Penance! Penance! Penance!"* And that same day water from the miraculous spring gushed forth.

On March 25th, the Lady revealed herself as the "Immaculate Conception." The assertion is obviously the central point of the Lourdes apparitions, just as the prayer: "Mary, conceived without sin," together with the Miraculous Medal, forms the essential element of the apparitions of the Rue du Bac.

The white robe and sky-blue girdle with which Mary is clothed, symbolize her integrity, the source of which is the absolute purity of her Immaculate Heart. Her joined hands are a call to prayer. To fight sensuality and the impiety of the day, the Blessed Virgin bids Bernadette to pray, and she, the Mother of God, prays with her. To all she recommends *penance,* the only means along with prayer to obtain pardon for men. This is the very basis of the devotion to Mary of which Lourdes has become the center. Side by side with her title of Immaculate, she reveals her SORROWFUL Heart.

IV

OUR LADY OF PONTMAIN

For the fourth time in forty years, Our Lady's feet touched the soil of France. She chose a small parish in the West, at the crossroads of the Catholic provinces of Brittany, Vendee and Normandy — PONTMAIN. During the preceding six months, France had waged a bloody war against Prussia, a war without possibility of an honorable peace. Paris was on the verge of capitulation: the country was gradually being overrun; the town of Laval would soon fall and, in consequence, the parish of Pontmain must needs, in turn, suffer enemy occupation.

It was then that Our Lady intervened. The evening of January 17, 1871, young Eugene Barbedette went out to see what the weather was like. Suddenly he saw over the house opposite his own a beautiful Lady who smiled to him. She wore a blue robe, and on it, over the place of her heart, a little red cross. On her head was a golden crown and a black veil. Within a short time more than eighty persons, amongst them the parish priest, were there and recited the Rosary. An inscription now appeared in the sky: "Pray, children!" and, immediately another: "God will soon give ear to your prayers: my Son will have pity." Eleven days afterwards, the nightmare of the war came to an end.

In the second phase of the apparition Mary held in her hands a crucifix, red like the cross which adorned her breast. She grasped it and lowered it towards the children Eugene and Joseph Barbedette, Francis Richet and Jeanne Marie Lebosse.

Once again Our Lady draws attention to her role of co-redemptrix — to her SORROWFUL Heart, which in order to show her pity for mankind has taken precedence over her Immaculate Heart.

The apparition of Pontmain takes on a national character. As a remedy against all the evils which threaten France it points to prayer and reparation for the expiation of sin and for the disarming of the hand of the Savior.

Thus its message is identical with that of La Salette which, to a great extent, has passed unheeded.

V

OUR LADY OF FATIMA

Our Lady was to remain silent for forty-six years. It is no longer to France, but to Portugal that she comes — Portugal now a victim of anti-Christian forces.

It was in 1917 — May 13th. The first World War, during which Portugal fought on the side of France, had already been in progress for three years.

Three little shepherds, Lucy, Francis and Jacinta had brought their flock into a valley called Cova da Iria. All of a sudden, in the midst of a brilliant light, they saw a beautiful Lady, bright as the sun. She wore a dazzling robe as white as snow. She smiled a little, but with a touch of sadness. Her hands were joined, a Rosary hung on her right arm.

That day and during the apparitions that followed, she stressed the necessity of making sacrifices; the acceptance of suffering; reparation and constant prayer. On June 13th, Mary, opening her hands, lifted the right hand which held the Rosary, in the attitude of one who blesses, and lowered the left hand to the level of her girdle. She thus gave them the vision of her Heart in the midst of thorns which "surrounded it on all sides." The points of these thorns penetrated the very veins of her Heart. And from this Heart rays of light projected downwards to the earth.

The Heart, surrounded and pierced with thorns, is certainly the symbol of the suffering endured by Mary in her Immaculate Heart which by this very fact, becomes a SORROWFUL Heart. This showing was very similar to that of the Divine Master who manifested Himself on December 27, 1673 to Saint Margaret Mary who beheld "irradiating on all sides, around His Heart a crown of thorns brighter than the sun and transparent as crystal."

During the last apparition at Fatima, on October 13th, the Blessed Virgin called herself "the Lady of the Rosary." She expressed her wish to have a chapel built on this spot and emphasized, as at La Salette, penance and the conversion of sinners, pointing out that they should no longer offend Our Lord "Who is already too much offended."

Her expression was "SORROWFUL." These were the last

words of the Mother of the Savior, preceding the great miracle of the sun.

While the crowd, breathless with emotion, contemplated this striking spectacle, the three children were gazing at four living pictures in succession — the Holy Family; Our Lord lovingly blessing the crowd; Our Lady of Dolors and Our Lady of Mount Carmel.

Anyone familiar with the visions and revelations given to the little seers of Fatima can hardly fail to see that they bear out in a striking way all that is implied in the Devotion to the Sorrowful and Immaculate Heart of Mary.

VI
OUR LADY OF BEAURAING
November 29, 1932 — January 3, 1933

On this occasion, it was Belgium that was the privileged soil with apparition after apparition.

The five children Fernande, Gilberte and Albert Voisin, Andrée and Gilberte Degeimbre perceived on leaving school a strange light and in its midst was a Lady dressed in white, holding a Rosary in her hand. She was crowned with rays. The Lady returned no less than thirty-four times. She asked for a chapel to which people might come on pilgrimage. She said: "I am the Immaculate Virgin. I am the Mother of God, the Queen of Heaven. I shall convert sinners. Do you love my Son?" "Yes, we do love Him," answered the children. "Do you love me?" "Yes, we do love you." "Then, sacrifice yourselves for me." It is always this idea of sacrifice, self-surrender, renunciation in everything. We must be victims with Mary, with Mary SORROWFUL at the foot of the Cross.

The essential part of the message of Beauraing consists in the showing of the heart of gold of the Mother of the Savior, for gold symbolizes purity; charity which is love; and glory.

VII
OUR LADY OF BANNEUX
1933

Banneux is the completion and prolongation of Beauraing. It is also like an echo of Lourdes. Eight times between January 15 and March 2, 1933, the Blessed Virgin showed herself to young Mariette Beco, as our "Lady of the Poor." No less than three times she asked for a "little Chapel." She insisted that people should pray much. A spring arose in the spot which she marked out, as she said: "Dip your hands into the water. This spring is reserved for me; it is for the people of every nation. Henceforth it is here that all who suffer may quench their thirst, whether it be of soul or body, for," she added, "I have come to relieve sufferings." As the Mother of Sorrows, who can have a deeper insight into suffering?

And this time she said: "Believe in me — I shall believe in you."

Yes, let us believe in her, in all the power of her SORROW-FUL and Immaculate Heart!

Vast throngs come to beg Our Lady of Banneux for courage to live their Christian lives and to be detached from the goods of this world. Year after year pilgrims come from Germany, Belgium, France and more especially from Holland to receive here the spirit of poverty and penance.

It is the triumph of the Golden Heart through penance!

VIII
OUR LADY OF TEARS OF SYRACUSE

In the house of a laborer of communistic and anti-clerical leanings, a plaster cast of the Madonna was seen to weep from August 29 to September 1, 1953. The plaque was hanging over a bed on which the wife of this man lay gravely ill.

Following all the due local investigation, and its subsequent examination by the authorities in Rome, the Bishops of Sicily unanimously declared that the marvel was beyond the sphere of natural cause and effect, and entirely worthy of credence. The tears were human tears. The number of cures and conversions continues to be impressive and a sanctuary is being built there.

We do not find here, as in the preceding manifestations, either visionaries or apparitions properly so called. It is certain that, apart from the miraculous cures, the event which provoked this surprising religious manifestation is not comparable to the rich background of apparitions in which messages of Our Lady were accompanied by visions from on high. Nevertheless, we cannot help being struck and deeply impressed by these tears which arise in the SORROWFUL Heart of a Mother weeping yet once more over the sins of the world and over the evils with which it is threatened. . .

* * *

These heavenly manifestations — which we are by no means bound to believe — are varied as to time, place and manner of happening. But all of them coincide in this — that they demonstrate the deep concern of the Mother of God for the conversion of sinners, and for the sanctification and salvation of souls. And this holds good in the case of the subject of this little book, *Devotion to the Sorrowful and Immaculate Heart of Mary.*

In matters concerning apparitions and revelations, the Church always imposes a testing time. If the showings have a divine origin, their genuineness will emerge, and their authenticity will be affirmed through the Vicar of Christ. It is thus in humble submission to this the Voice of Christ on earth, that we await the universal triumph of the DEVOTION OF THE SORROWFUL AND IMMACULATE HEART OF MARY.

APPENDIX

In India, Devotion to the Sorrowful and Immaculate Heart of Mary began in 1952 through the instrumentality of Father Louis M. Shouriah, S.J. He was miraculously cured by Our Lady in circumstances that are not without interest. We give his own account: —

"I had been suffering for three years from grave heart trouble. The case was at length declared hopeless by the medical men, two of whom had actually numbered the days of my life. Feeling disconsolate, I prayed ardently to the Mother of Sorrows: 'My most sweet Mother, you know how much I am suffering physically and mentally, and how ready I am to endure all in union with your own sufferings and sorrows. If my sufferings are destined to do good to souls obtain for me strength and courage to bear them. Otherwise, I beg you to take me away from this world, for I do not wish to be a burden to others.' "

"It was February 11, 1952, Feast of Our Lady of Lourdes, and Titular of the little church of which I was the parish priest. That day my novena ended, and I was anxious to say Mass. I reached the altar by the support of two people: but I came away from it, unaided, with the joy of feeling that my youth had been renewed!"

"I could not explain this extraordinary change, for it was beyond my comprehension. Immediately after the elevation, I experienced a heavenly joy, and I felt my health fully restored. I was cured miraculously at the moment when our Lady whispered to me from the big statue above the altar: 'YOU ARE CURED.' It seemed incredible, but I was feeling all the signs of perfect health. I was overwhelmed with confusion!"

"During my thanksgiving — wondering still if the cure was real — I asked our Blessed Mother how I could best show my gratitude for this unsolicited favor. Like a flash of lightning came the whisper: 'You are cured of this disease, but you will have to suffer in other ways for my sake. I am with you. Are you ready?' With tears of joy, I prostrated myself and I gave my willing consent. At this moment, the statue of Our Lady of Lourdes came down from its niche high above the altar. Coming to life, it stood by my side saying in a clear voice: 'Spread the Devotion to my Sorrowful and Immaculate Heart in your country. To this end, pious souls will arise to help you.' "

"I raised my head, but before I could open my eyes, our Lady was gone! Since that happy day, I am spending myself for this one special object despite many sufferings and sorrows. Our Lady smiles upon me, and helps me to endure all with joy."

"The remarkable thing is that never till that day had I heard or read of the Devotion to the Sorrowful and Immaculate Heart of Mary. But relying on the words of our Lady I placed my entire confidence in her, and with the approval of my ecclesiastical superiors I set to work. I can attest that every one of Our Lady's words concerning my sufferings "in other ways" and the spontaneous help of "pious souls" is being literally fulfilled."

"Strange circumstances in various parts of the world have brought all this about. I came in contact with the Belgian Center of the Devotion: and I got to know the life of Berthe Petit, the apostle of the Sorrowful and Immaculate Heart of Mary. I prepared a small book for publication entitled 'A Message of World-Wide Importance — Devotion to the Sorrowful and Immaculate Heart of Mary.' I wrote articles in various Catholic magazines, and I issued leaflets and prayers for the Devotion in the English, Tamil, Telugu, Malayan, Conarese and Indian languages. The "Decade of the Rosary" Crusade for the conversion of sinners is proving a great success. The "Art of Divine Love: Berthe Petit" is spread through every country of the world, more especially in the U.S.A., through the efforts of Fr. John Ryan, S.J., the Editor of *Fatima Findings*. Thus our Lady has taken my whole life into her service. To work for her: to write of her: to compassionate her in her sorrows: to help others to know and love her — all this is such an other-worldly labor of love that I could not call it 'work.' "

(Editor's Note. — Father Shouriah, S.J., died on May 26, 1958, following a heart attack, and in the midst of preparation for a pilgrimage to Europe which was to include a visit of thanksgiving to the grave of Berthe Petit and attendance at the sessions of a Marian Congress in Lourdes.)

INDEX

Propaganda Mariana, 99
Prov. of Liege, 95
Prussia, 106
Pyrenees, 105
Quebec, 99
Queen Elisabeth of the
    Belgians, 72
Queen of Heaven, 80, 105,
    108
Quito, 100
Rabat, 99
Redemptorist Fathers of
    Saigon, 101
religious vocation, 1
Reunion Islands, 101
Rev. Fr. Bainvel, 42
Rev. Fr. Hermann Morin, 99
Rev. Fr. Ryan, 100
Reverend Dom Manuel
    Cordoso, 98
Reverend Dr. Godbout, 99
Reverend Father Tesnière, 4
Revue Biblique, 42
rheumatism, 7, 67, 81
Rhine, 12
Roger O'Brien, 99
Rome, 9, 19, 21, 29, 32, 34,
    35, 40, 59, 98, 109
Rosary Basilica, 22
Ruanda, 101
rue Archimede, 98
Rue des Cendres, 60
Rue du Bac, 103, 105
Rue du Cornet, 10, 53
rue Guimard, 87
Rue Jordaens, 64
Rue Joseph Stallaert, 66, 67,
    70, 82
Rue Rogier, 60
Sacred College, 33
Sacred Heart of Jesus, 34
Saigon, 101
Saint Catherine of Siena, 21
Saint Joseph, 58
Saint Teresa, 76
Salazié, 101
Sarajevo, 27
Sarnen, 27, 29, 48
Sarnten, 69
Secretariat de la Devotion, 87
Sicily, 10, 109

Siena, 21, 23, 76, 84
Simba, 101
Sirkali Mission, 102
Sister M. Madeleine, 8
Sisters of Charity, 67, 103
Sisters of Charity of Ghent, 67
Sisters of Good Hope of
    Binche, 61
Sisters of Nevers, 66
Sisters of St. Thomas of
    Villanova, 48
Sisters of St. Vincent de Paul,
    2
Sisters of the Sacred Heart, 53
Sisters of the Union of the
    Sacred Hearts, 1
Society of the African
    Missions, 87
Sorrowful and Immaculate
    Heart of Mary, 32, 36, 89,
    94, 95, 96, 100, 101, 112
Soul, 100
Spain, 94, 97
Sr. Joseph of the Sacred
    Heart, 51
Sr. Valesine, 51
St. Bernadette's Hospital, 66
St. Catherine of Siena, 20, 71
St. Francis of Assisi, 74
St. Gudule, 95
St. John, 15, 16, 18, 84
St. Joseph, 25, 34
St. Louis College, 60
St. Mark's, 10
St. Michael, 20
St. Paul, 8, 77
St. Pius X, 11
St. Quentin, 18
St. Vincent de Paul, 4
Switzerland, 12, 27, 29, 32,
    46, 51, 53, 60, 69, 74, 93,
    94, 97, 98
Syracuse, 103
Tamil, 112
Tanjore, 102
Telugu, 112
Teresa of the Child Jesus, 56
The Crusade of the Decade,
    102
The Blue Army, 98, 100
Third Order of St. Dominic, 21

Secret of the Rosary

Publications

Printed in the USA
CPSIA information can be obtained
at www.ICGtesting.com
LVHW090604120324
774158LV00002B/332